A Futurist for the 21st Century

The Macrohistory of Lawrence Taub (1936-2018)

Edited by Jan Krikke

DCO Books

"I regard Taub's ideas as similar to those archetypes of human behavior and group behavior present in the Chinese Book of Changes, the I Ching, from the first millennium BC. The I Ching is a very interesting and useful book of consultancy and advice for people even today – not because of any mysterious external esoteric spirits or such, but because it is a tool that helps unlock different viewpoints from within one's own mind…

"I suggest that there exist ancient archetypical mind patterns which are useful even today. Some of them are apparent in Taub's three models. Science is not the sole source of knowledge, nor is scientific knowledge exhaustive and exclusive. Futures research as well as scientific knowledge calls for widening the scope and meaning of scientific knowledge so that it would also include interpretational knowledge of history and perceptional knowledge of the future in addition to the objective knowledge of the present."

Prof. Dr. Pentti Malaska (RIP), former Finland Futures Research Centre and former President of the World Futures Studies Federation

CONTENTS

Preface

This collection of essays is a tribute to Lawrence (Larry) Taub, the American macrohistorian and author of the book *The Spiritual Imperative: Sex, Age, and the Last Caste.*

Taub developed a distinctive macro-historical model that transcends a purely Western perspective and takes Asian history into account, resulting in a more holistic, global view of humanity's evolution.

The book features contributions from six different authors. Jan Krikke, editor of the second edition of Taub's book, wrote a summary of Taub's macrohistory.

Professor Sohail Inayatullah, Chair in Futures Studies at UNESCO, explains the distinctions between Taub's caste model and a similar model from Indian spiritual teacher R.P. Sarkar.

Bill Kelly, former lecturer in communications studies at UCLA, who wrote the foreword to Taub's book, provides an intimate essay on Taub's life and legacy.

Also included is a review of Taub's macrohistory, written by futurist scholar Takuya Murata for the journal *Futures* of the Hawaii Research Center for Futures Studies at the University of Hawaii.

We hear Taub's own voice in an interview he gave to the P2P Foundation and in a summary of his macrohistory he presented at the 15th World Futures Study Federation (WFSF) Conference in Brisbane in 2001.

Lastly, we hear from Masanori Kanda, the Japanese business management expert who wrote the foreword to the Japanese edition of Taub's book. Mr. Kanda captures the unique personality and character of Lawrence Taub.

The original 11 illustrations from *The Spiritual Imperative* are included in this volume.

Introduction

Macrohistorian Lawrence (Larry) Taub wrote *The Spiritual Imperative: Sex, Age, and the Last Caste* while living in Tokyo. The book was translated into Japanese and quickly climbed to the top of Japan's bestseller list. It was later translated into Korean and Spanish. However, the English edition struggled to gain traction in the West, likely due to Taub's unique macrohistorical perspective, which blends the worldviews of India, Europe, and China.

Most macrohistories focus on a particular domain—economics, technology, religion, or ideology. Taub's work is distinctive in that it integrates three different "coordinates"—sex (gender), age, and caste—each representing a distinct dimension of human development.

At the heart of Taub's macrohistory is the Caste Model, which should not be confused with the Caste System. The word "caste" is a European distortion of the Sanskrit term varna, which means "color." In ancient Vedic literature, varna was central to a prophecy about the cyclical nature of history.

The Vedic sages identified four key human traits or natural inclinations—aptitudes we might today describe as "a born salesman" or "a natural leader." The four varnas are teacher, protector, trader, and worker. While every individual possesses elements of all four traits, one typically dominates in each person, regardless of gender. The sages predicted that humanity passes through cycles in which different varnas hold global prominence. Taub mapped this varna cycle onto the course of human history, using his Caste Model to explain shifts in regional preeminence, such as the current rise of the East.

Taub was not the first to explore the varna cycle. The modern Indian spiritual teacher P.R. Sarkar based his social development theories on this cycle, and Sohail Inayatullah, Chair in Futures Studies at UNESCO, incorporates it into his master classes. Inayatullah also collaborated with Australian scholars to develop the Sarkar Game, a tool used in corporate training to promote collaboration across different organizational ranks.

The second key element of Taub's macrohistory is the Sex Model, which addresses the role of women in major historical transitions. According to Taub, the female principle was dominant in prehistory, suppressed during the Patriarchal Age, and reemerged in the 20th century. He predicted that the 21st century would see the androgynous integration of the male and the female principles.

The third component of Taub's macrohistory, the Age Model, posits that history evolves in stages of spiritual development that mirror the life stages of an individual. Taub suggested that humanity progressed through phases such as the Age of Birth, the Age of Infancy, and the Age of Early Childhood. This idea echoes the evolutionary theory of "ontogeny recapitulates phylogeny" from Ernst Haeckel, as well as concepts discussed by Sigmund Freud in *Totem and Taboo*. Taub also argued that this model underpins much of the work of Integral theorist Ken Wilber.

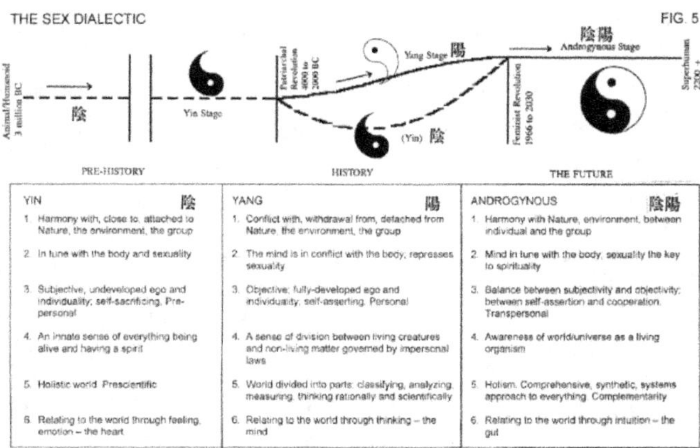

YIN 陰	YANG 陽	ANDROGYNOUS 陰陽
1. Harmony with, close to, attached to Nature, the environment, the group	1. Conflict with, withdrawal from, detached from Nature, the environment, the group	1. Harmony with Nature, environment, between individual and the group
2. In tune with the body and sexuality	2. The mind is in conflict with the body; represses sexuality	2. Mind in tune with the body; sexuality the key to spirituality
3. Subjective, undeveloped ego and individuality; self-sacrificing. Pre-personal	3. Objective; fully-developed ego and individuality; self-asserting. Personal	3. Balance between subjectivity and objectivity; between self-assertion and cooperation. Transpersonal
4. An innate sense of everything being alive and having a spirit	4. A sense of division between living creatures and non-living matter governed by impersonal laws	4. Awareness of world/universe as a living organism
5. Holistic world. Prescientific	5. World divided into parts: classifying, analyzing, measuring, thinking rationally and scientifically	5. Holism. Comprehensive, synthetic, systems approach to everything. Complementarity
6. Relating to the world through feeling, emotion – the heart	6. Relating to the world through thinking – the mind	6. Relating to the world through intuition – the gut

Taub believed that the Age Model could be applied broadly to nations and regions, with Northern Europe representing the "oldest" or most mature region, given its advanced social development and gender equality.

While Taub's predictions were often off by decades, the strength of his work lies in the models themselves. They reveal what he called the "deeper currents" of history—sex, age, and caste—that shape humanity across cultures, religions, and ideologies. These currents help explain many of the seemingly contradictory developments in today's world.

* * *

Part 1
The Macrohistory of Lawrence Taub

Jan Krikke

"It is important to recognize that, in theory, Varna is non-genealogical. The four Varnas are not lineages, but categories."
Alf Hiltebeitel, Professor of Religion at George Washington University

Larry Taub belonged to a generation of 20th-century futurists that include the likes of Alvin Toffler, Samuel Huntington, Francis Fukuyama, and Paul Kennedy. Futurists, or macrohistorians, look at deeper currents and fault lines in human history to anticipate probable future scenarios. Alvin Toffler's landmark book *Future Shock* showed that humanity moved from a hunter-gatherer to an agricultural, to an industrial, and finally to a post-industrial society. Francis Fukuyama's *The End of History* argued that Western liberal democracy had won the ideological battle with communism after the fall of the Berlin Wall, and Samuel Huntington's *The Clash of Civilizations and the Remaking of World Order* asserted that cultural and religious identities would be the primary source of conflict in the post-Cold War world.

Taub's macrohistory stands out for several reasons. Conventional macrohistory usually relies on one parameter, whether that is politics, economics, technology, or religion. It will tell us what is likely to happen in the future, but it tends to be vague about dates and geographic specifics (time and space). Taub developed a macrohistory that deals not only with economics and politics, but also with gender, culture, spirituality, and consciousness, and he is specific about developments in geographical areas. His Sex Model details the crucial role women will play in the near future, the Age Model deals with evolving human maturity, and the Caste Model, Taub's interpretation of the Indian philosophy of history, addresses the evolution of human consciousness.

The catalyst for Taub's macrohistory was India. While visiting the country in the 1970s, he learned about the Varna, the basis for the socio-spiritual organization of ancient Hindu society. The notion of *Varna*, which later degenerated into the much-maligned caste system, shaped India's social structure the way Confucianism shaped China's social structure. Varna has been translated as type, order, and color. Portuguese explorers mispronounced Varna as "casta," and the word was later Anglicized as "caste." While the caste system that developed in later centuries resembles a division of labor and is tied to birth, the original notion of Varna is based on *Karma* and *Guna*. *Karma* means conduct, deeds, occupation, and accomplishments. *Guna* means qualities, attributes, virtues, or character. Varna had no restrictions regarding a person moving from one Varna to another.

The Indian sages who conceived the concept of Varna used what must be the earliest form of psychological profiling. They argued that humans can be grouped into four "generic" types based on their Karma and Guna:

- Spiritual types: those who enlighten others, such as educators and administrators (*Brahman*). They value their mind as their greatest asset and use it to develop spiritual reality, and knowledge of science, and to make rules and laws enforced by the warrior. They strive for enlightenment and lead others by furthering religion or spiritual development.

- Protectors: those who thrive on competition, value physical strength, and protect others (*Kshatriya*). They emphasize courage, honor, discipline, and sacrifice. They protect society from danger and chaos by maintaining order. They obey authority and follow orders, and expect others to do the same.

- Merchants: those who value material possessions and excel in efficiency, managing money, administration, and organization (*Vaishya*). They are efficient and can effectively manage others to produce goods and achieve complex tasks, advancing the material well-being of society.

- Workers: those who take pride in their work and empathize with and nourish others. They value mundane pleasures, safety, security, and reasonable comforts. They leave political and economic decisions to leaders from other castes, but they can bring the system down if their needs are not met.

Taub points out that each individual typically has traits of two or more caste types. A worker can also have merchant inclinations, and a warrior type can also have spiritual leanings. But one of the four caste types usually dominates in each individual. To the ancient Indian sages, the four caste types are mutually dependent. All were needed for society to function. Warriors provided protection, merchants delivered the goods, spiritual types offered guidance, and workers did the heavy lifting. There was no hierarchy until, as prominent yogi Sadhguru pointed out, "the goldsmith started to feel superior to the blacksmith."

The Indian caste differs from the European notion of class. The word "class" is etymologically derived from the Latin "classis." Roman census takers used the term *classis* to categorize citizens by wealth to determine military service obligations. In the 16th century, class got an economic connotation to denote the difference between the landed aristocracy, the bourgeoisie, and merchants on the one hand, and farmers, laborers, and servants on the other. In the 19th century, Marxism gave class its socioeconomic connotation, and in the 20th century, social scientists in the US used the term to distinguish between upper and lower classes based on wealth or income.

The notion of varna has its origin in Indian cosmology. The Sanskrit classics outline a "cosmic macrohistory" based on the cyclical notion of time. According to sages, humanity goes through four ages (*yuga*) during which the four castes take turns "ruling the world." That is to say, one of the four castes is dominant at a given age until it is replaced by another caste. This caste cycle repeats itself eternally. During the first caste age of each cycle, the dominant caste is the Spiritual-Religious caste, followed by the warriors, the merchants, and the workers, after which the cycle starts again with the Spiritual-Religious caste. To make this cycle run smoothly, humans have to fulfill their *dharma* (duty) according to their Varna. Following one's *dharma* is the path to attaining enlightenment and reaching Nirvana, the highest state of being or consciousness a person can achieve.

The Hindu sages used cosmic, rather than human, time frames. A *yuga*, or caste age, is a unit of time consisting of five solar years. Four *yugas* make up the *mahayuga* (great *yuga*) and 2,000 *mahayugas* make up the cosmic cycle, the *kalpa*. Caste ages become successively shorter. According to the Sanskrit scriptures, the first *yuga* (*Krita*, first Spiritual Caste Age), lasted 1,728,000 years. The current *yuga* (*Kali*), began in 3102 BCE and will last for 432,000 years. At the end of the *Kaliyuga*, the world will be destroyed, to be recreated after a period of quiescence before the cycle begins again.

Caste Cycles and History

In a remarkable intuitive leap, Taub discarded the cosmic time frames referred to by the Hindu sages. He concluded that the caste cycle can be mapped on actual human history—to specific historical periods (time) and specific geographic regions (space). His Caste Model follows the sequence predicted by Sanskrit scriptures—Spiritual Age, Warrior Age, Merchant Age, and Worker Age—but rather than a new cycle starting over again after the destruction of the world (alluded to in Sanskrit scriptures), Taub sees the current *Kaliyuga* as the prelude to a new Spiritual Age, which he calls Spiritual-Religious Age II.

Figure 3 is Taub's Caste Model in a nutshell. It is juxtaposed with his Sex Model. The upper part of the figure shows the caste cycle in time, and the lower part shows the caste cycle in space. In the Caste Model, prehistory was the first Spiritual Age. Animism was the global "religion" of the world. It was a time of shamans, witches, and belief in supernatural powers. Next came the Warrior Age, marked by great warriors like Alexander the Great, Ajatasatru, and Genghis Khan. Central to their life were combat and armies. Their ruling elite were kings, nobility, and generals, their social ideal was the hero, and their source of power was land.

The last great power of the Warrior Age was Spain with its *conquistadors*. They were superseded in the 17th century by the Dutch, the pioneers of the Merchant Age. Merchant Caste trade and exploitation replaced Warrior Caste conquest and plunder. The Dutch developed the prototype for the modern multinational (the East India Company); they opened the world's first stock exchange and had the world's first reserve currency. In Holland and elsewhere, power shifted from combat to money, financiers replaced generals as the ruling elite, and the *Hero* of the Warrior Age was superseded by the *Self-Made Man* of the Merchant Age.

THE CASTE MODEL · FIG. 3

THE FIVE CASTE AGES		SANSKRIT NAME	TIME
	(animal)		
1. Spiritual-Religious Age No. 1		Satyayuga I	3 million to 4000/2000 BC
2. Warrior Age		Tretayuga	4000/2000 BC to early 17th Century AD
3. Merchant Age		Dvaparayuga	c. 1650 to c. 1975
4. Worker Age		Kaliyuga	c. 1917 to c. 2030
5. Spiritual-Religious Age No. 2		Satyayuga II	c. 1979 to Superhumanity
	(superhuman)		

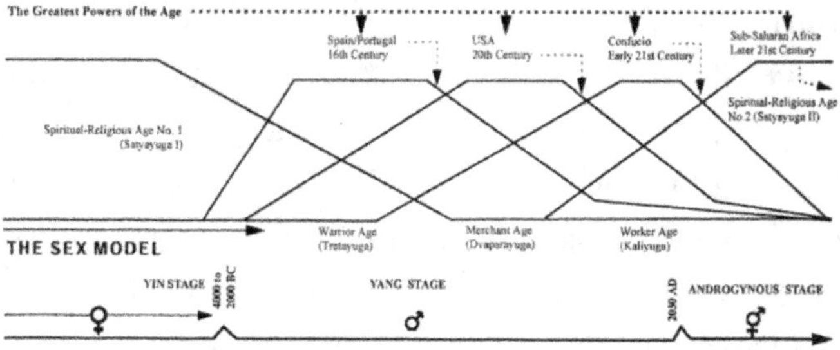

Remnants of the Warrior Age survive today as royalty and military honor guards. Remnants of the lingering Merchant Age survive in the form of capital concentration, tax havens, and corporate monopolies. But most industrialized countries are firmly in the Worker Age. The vast majority of people are working for a wage or a salary, and their identity is closely tied to their work. In the Warrior and Merchant Ages, the family name, land holdings, money, and wealth defined one's status in society. Today, most people are defined by and identify with their work or profession. "What kind of work do you do?" is commonly the first question when people meet for the first time. Even presidents and prime ministers have "job approval" ratings.

Taub's three materialist caste ages are similar to those of Marx: the Warrior Age is feudalism, the Merchant Age is capitalism, and the Worker Age is socialism. Marxism as a political ideology played a key role in the early phase of the Worker Age (see Fig. 9). While it had enormous political impact and paved the way for "socialist" governments (social democracies), Taub explains why Marxism didn't endure. First, it defined "working class" too narrowly, referring mainly to blue-collar wage labor. In Taub's Caste Model, workers include anyone working for a wage, salary, fee, or "nothing," such as most peasants, professionals, white-collar workers, serfs, and women doing housework and childcare.

Another defect in the Marxist model is its economic determinism—the assumption that economics is the determining factor in all historical periods. Taub notes that the Marxist model shows this bent by naming all of its stages of history by their socioeconomic systems: slavery, feudalism, capitalism, etc. This defect led Marx to make faulty predictions because there are deeper determining forces in history aside from economic ones.

"Marx, Engels, and their followers," Taub writes, "lived in one of the two most economically determined and economically focused of the caste ages: the Merchant Age. Moreover, they pioneered the development of the other: the Worker Age. So they easily fell into the trap of thinking that all ages were and must be equally economically determined." He refers to the Iranian Revolution that shocked the Western world. Its force was religious rather than economic.

Caste Struggle

Taub distinguishes two successive economic systems in each caste age. The first predominates during the caste's early revolutionary-evolutionary stage, and the second predominates during its later peak stage.

<u>Spiritual-Religious Age No. 1:</u>
1. Paleolithic: hunting, gathering, fishing, and herding
2. Meso-Neolithic: horticulture, agriculture, and livestock raising

Warrior Age
1. Slavery
2. Feudalism

Merchant Age
1. Commercial-mercantile capitalism: trade, hand-manufacture, early industry
2. Industrial capitalism: machine manufacture, full industrialization

Worker Age
1. Communism, or socialism
2. Social-democratic, multinational corporate capitalism, or Japanese-style worker-caste "teamwork" capitalism

<u>Spiritual-Religious Age No. 2 (the future)</u>
1. Religious or spiritual capitalism: machines do drudge work (physical and mental); humans do creative work
2. Anarchist, integrated economy: human and machine integrated

Caste struggle is not merely about power. It is also about the evolution of human consciousness. Taub notes that the Warrior

Age introduced the horrors of large-scale war and sexual and class oppression on a scale unknown in the preceding Spiritual-Religious Age No. 1. However, it also allowed trade to flourish, and promoted reason and science, while the conquests of warrior emperors like Constantine and Ashoka spread advanced spiritual consciousness to the masses through Christianity and Buddhism. The Merchant Age brought the evils of capitalism, commercialism, and urban industrial blight, but also ended slavery and raised the level of material well-being among the masses.

The current Worker Age similarly has upsides and downsides. "It is an age of both great spiritual and material development," Taub writes. "It is the first age to reject war and imperialism, to try world government, to deeply embrace equality, to cause science and technology to flower, and to create material wealth and security for the masses. But it is also the notorious *Kaliyuga* [i.e. the last of the four caste ages before the new Spiritual-Religious Caste Age]. It is the most socially alienated, materialistic, spiritually dark and dismal, complicated, disorienting, and dangerous of all caste ages. It is, in short, the best and worst of all possible worlds so far."

In Taub's Caste Model, the West dominated the Merchant Age, because its worldview most closely aligned with Merchant Caste values. Similarly, Confucian East Asia will dominate the peak stage of the Worker Age because its worldview most closely aligns with the Worker Caste. While the US has also moved into the Worker Age, it is the last great power of the Merchant Age. It struggles to rid itself of its ingrained Merchant Caste worldview. It stresses rights and freedom at the expense of responsibility and civil obligation. Donald J. Trump was the last US president to openly espouse a Merchant Caste worldview.

Taub predicts that the Worker Age will reach its zenith in East Asia between 2030 and 2040. Confucian East Asia, with its collectivist societies, is most in tune with the values, ideals, and socioeconomic worldview of the Worker Caste (see Fig. 1). Japan, China, Taiwan, and Korea have different political systems, but their "teamwork capitalism" has put them in the vanguard of the Fourth Industrial Revolution (or Industry 4.0). East Asia has the additional advantage that it is not held back by strong remnants of the Merchant Age. In many Western countries, Merchant Caste oligarchs have an outsized influence on the government;

in China, the government controls the oligarchs.

Rising Spiritual-Religious Caste

The previous Merchant Age and the current Worker Age have one thing in common: materialism. While materialism has a negative connotation, we can distinguish between mindless consumption and an ostentatious display of wealth on the one hand, and the human need for material goods like shelter, food, and sanitation on the other. The Worker Age is well on its way to providing all of humanity with material necessities. China lifted the majority of its 1.3 billion people out of poverty in just a few decades. India, South-East Asia, and Africa are on track to do the same.

Many developing countries use the formula China has applied: central control in combination with (managed) market liberalization. UN agencies and other international bodies hope to eradicate global poverty (living on an income of less than $2 per day) by 2030. China, as the world's largest producer and main power in the Worker Age, plays a key role in this process. Chinese products, technology, and investment are flowing to developing countries that strive to provide people with necessities—if not Western material lifestyles.

The Worker Caste has yet to reach its peak stage in East Asia, which will be around 2040. But the next caste age, Spiritual-Religious Caste Age No. 2, has already made its presence felt. Taub calls it the Spiritual-Religious Caste Age to distinguish between religion and spirituality. Religions tend to focus on beliefs, while spirituality is concerned with "the search within." Interest in spirituality in the West began in the late 19th century when Madame Blavatsky founded the Theosophical Society and Vedanta Societies that first sprang up in the US. In Europe, the pioneers of quantum physics explored Eastern spirituality. But the trend reached critical mass in the 1960s. The hippies embraced spirituality, and interest in Eastern thought exploded. A journey to India became a rite of passage for many of the hippie generation.

By the mid-1970s, the movement transformed into the New Age movement, which explored everything from Indian spirituality to Gnosticism. Unbelievers became seekers. Millions of people in industrialized countries started practicing yoga, meditation, and other consciousness-raising techniques. The movement spread through all levels of society. By the 1980s, corporate mindfulness training and meditation classes became a growth industry.

The 1960s also saw the birth of new religious movements that split from traditional established religions. Mega churches and TV evangelists attracted millions of people. The Unification Church in Korea had millions of followers around the world. In Japan, *Seichō no Ie* ("House of Growth"), was one of several "New Thought" religions. It emphasized gratitude for nature, family, ancestors, and religious faith in one universal God. China saw the birth of the *Falun Gong* (Dharma Wheel Practice), a mixture of Chinese and Indian thought that combines meditation and qigong exercises.

Fundamentalism

New Age spirituality, alternative religions, and religious fundamentalism seem to be strange bedfellows, but in the Caste Model, they are part of the same caste struggle. This explains why Taub marks the 1979 Iranian Revolution as the start of the Spiritual-Religious Age No. 2. Iran skipped the Merchant Age and jumped from the Warrior Age straight into the next Spiritual-Religious Age. The catalyst for this "caste age skipping" was Western interference.

In the early 1950s, Iran elected its first democratic government, headed by Mohammad Mosaddegh. The Iranian government nationalized British oil assets and a dispute over compensation led to a British-US intervention, which ended the first Islamic experiment with a democratic government. The Western powers deposed Mohammad Mosaddegh and installed Mohammad Reza Pahlavi, better known as the Shah of Iran. Pahlavi had his roots in the Warrior Caste and used torture and other Warrior Age methods to stay in power.

The Middle East has retained many features of the Warrior Age. Most countries in the region are governed by sheiks and emirs, hereditary leftovers from the Warrior Age. Decades of Western support of these Warrior Caste leaders may cause other countries in the region to follow Iran's lead, using Islam as liberation theology. In the 1980s, Taub pointed at Egypt. Today he may have added Afghanistan, Yemen, Iraq, Syria, and perhaps bigger fish like Turkey and Pakistan. The West, stuck in its singular worldview, is still unable to imagine that a revolution can be fueled by religious fervor. As Taub wrote:

"Western countries are rooted in economic determinism, which is rooted in caste history.

In the Merchant and Worker Ages, people are motivated by economics. Most time and energy go into making a living to survive and/or worrying about it, piling up money and material wealth, or just working to fill the spiritual void. Since this motivation is so deeply ingrained, people assume that everyone else and every other is/was motivated in the same way. This projection is why Western governments can neither understand nor effectively deal with countries like Iran and movements like Islamic fundamentalism."

Taub did predict that more countries in the "religious belt" will follow Iran's path. He writes: "This all-pervasive religiousness in the religious belt explains why worker (socialist-communist) revolution never caught on in these religious-belt countries during the Worker Age. Socialism, communism, and other worker ideologies were too secular, materialistic, and atheistic for them. China could become a modern power through communist revolution, but not its likewise overpopulated neighbor, India." He added that even India may follow a similar path: "India, it seems, cannot act unless the action is religiously driven. But once it is, watch out!"

Religious fundamentalism is now a global phenomenon, and so is the search for personal spiritual growth. Taub predicted that these two seemingly disparate developments will eventually merge. Revolutions are fueled by extremism but become more accommodating once the revolutionary fever dies down. As Spiritual-Religious Caste Age 2 evolves, it will bring new values, new economic systems, new institutions, and a new worldview. Most importantly, women will play a key role in this evolution. They will restore the balance between the sexes that was lost during the masculine Warrior and Merchant Ages.

Age and Sex Models

The Caste Model is buttressed by the Age Model and the Sex Model. The Age Model, arguably the soft spot in Taub's macrohistory, is based on one main assumption, namely that the spiritual development of humanity as a whole parallels that of a single individual as he or she ages. The model distinguishes five basic periods from prehistory to the present age (see Fig. 7).

The infancy of humanity, which lasted until about 12,000 years ago, was a time when the human race was still part of nature, with no sense of a center, or individual self. This age corresponds to the newborn, when the child is unconscious of itself as a separate individual being. The baby subsequently recognizes that the world revolves around the mother. In early childhood, it attempts to get its wishes carried out by pleasing the mother, just as during late prehistory and early history, people tried to placate Great Mother Earth, the Goddess, to get their desires fulfilled. But as the father instead of the mother becomes the center of the individual's existence, the worship of the Father in Heaven replaces that of the Earth Mother. This is the time of later childhood and early adolescence.

For the past several hundred years in the West, secularized societies have gradually come into existence as God the Father is no longer acknowledged as the supreme authority. This historical period corresponds to the rejection of parental authority as the adolescent desires to assert his or her will in opposition to the parents. In 1851, British writer George Holyoake coined the word "secularism" to describe his views of promoting a social order separate from religion, without actively dismissing or criticizing religious belief.

Today we are at the late teenage stage, in which rebellious impulses predominate over the desire for autonomy, and we have yet to establish a well-grounded adult identity based on inner authority. Taub thinks that this "adult identity" may ultimately arise from an awareness of cosmic consciousness, i.e. humanity's experience of a unified and unbounded Self. This vision resembles that of the Eastern traditions and contrasts with the outlook of the Western monotheistic religions that worship a God conceived as a person transcendent to the individual soul.

The basic idea of the Age Model is not new. It is thought that Blaise Pascal first spoke of it in the 17th century. The evolution theorist Ernst Haeckel's "ontogeny recapitulates phylogeny" is a biological version of it. Sigmund Freud refers to it in *Totem and Taboo*, and it is the underlying premise for Ken Wilber's works on historical development. Taub uses the Age Model to show the dynamics of humanity's transition from religion to spirituality. Humanity has nearly outgrown its patriarchally-oriented religions and is entering adulthood. It will no longer look "outside" to religious guidance, but within—the deity manifests in the Self.

The Sex Model divides history and the future into three ages of human "sexual" development. The first was the Yin Age of prehistory, when humanity lived according to the female principle. The second was the Yang Age, covering most of recorded history until the present, when humanity moved to a worldview in tune with the male principle. The third age is the Androgynous Age, which started roughly in the middle of the 20th century, when humanity started to recapture lost "female" elements that the Yang Age repressed or "forgot," in order to achieve a balance between the female and male principles (see Fig. 5).

Taub's Sex Model was inspired by his friend Shulamith Firestone, the American feminist and author of *The Dialect of Sex: The Case for Feminist Revolution*. Firestone's book, first published in 1970, is a classic in feminist literature. She argued that the "sexual class system" runs far deeper and is far more damaging than the social and economic divide addressed by Marxism. Sexual oppression dates back to the age of the patriarchs and was institutionalized by religions for 2000 years.

The birth of feminism coincided with the rise of the Worker Age in the 19th and early 20th centuries. The word "feminism" was coined in the 1960s, but the movement began in the early 19th century, when women demanded the right to vote. In 1949, French author Simone de Beauvoir gave a boost to the feminist movement with her book *The Second Sex,* which outlined the history of female oppression, and in 1963, American author Betty Friedan's *The Feminine Mystique* challenged the male-imposed view that women had only one path to fulfillment: being a housewife and mother. The so-called second wave of feminism, at its height in the 1970s, fought for equal legal and social rights for women. Its leading theorists were Kate Millett (*Sexual Politics*, 1970) and Shulamith Firestone (*The Dialectic of Sex: The Case for Feminist Revolution*, 1970.)

Written when she was just 25, Firestone's *The Dialectic of Sex* is a feminist macrohistory in itself, as well as a cry from the heart. She wrote: "The first women are fleeing the massacre, and sharing and tottering, are beginning to find each other. Their first move is a careful joint observation, to resensitize a fractured consciousness. This is painful: no matter how many levels of consciousness one reaches, the problem always goes deeper. It is everywhere. The division yin and yang pervades all culture, history, economics, nature itself; modern Western versions of sex discrimination are only the most recent layer."

Taub was strongly influenced by *The Dialect of Sex*, but he went a step further by giving her feminist history a cultural dimension. Using the Chinese generic types of yin and yang that

Firestone had used, Taub argued that most cultures in prehistory had been matriarchies with yin characteristics. During the Warrior Age, societies in general became more yang, but Asia retained more of the yin features of the animist, pre-Warrior Caste Age. Eastern and Western religions reflect this distinction. Taub writes:

"The three main Western world religions, Judaism, Christianity, and Islam, are much more yang than the three main Eastern world religions, Hinduism, Hinayana Buddhism, and Mahayana Buddhism. Eastern cultures went through the same basic yang evolution as Western ones but retained many yin characteristics from prehistory. In the East, yin and yang features coexisted with relatively equal force – although juxtaposed rather than integrated. As a result, the intense conflict between yin and yang, and the strong repression of yin by yang, that typified Western cultures was less pronounced in the East."

Taub and Sarkar

When Taub arrived in India in the mid-1960s, his first stop was an ashram (a spiritual hermitage or a monastery in Indian religions) in Jamalpur on the Ganges in Bihar State. It was the home base of Prabhat Ranjan Sarkar, a guru, philosopher, author, and scientist. Sarkar founded Ananda Marga (the Path of Bliss), a spiritual and social organization that offers instruction in meditation and yoga. Unknown to Taub at the time, Sarkar had used the theory of caste to develop a socioeconomic and political theory called PROUT (Progressive Utilization Theory). PROUT combines socialism and spirituality based on collaboration and decentralization. While influenced by Marxism, it aims to address the shortcomings of both capitalism and communism. Showing its Indian (Vedanta) influence, PROUT encompasses the whole of the individual and collective existence for all beings, including physical, educational, mental, cultural, and spiritual.

Taub met Sarkar in 1966 when he was in India for a two-year stay. He recalled the meeting in an article for the *World Futures Studies Federation* magazine in 2009. "Mr. Sarkar wore many hats - spiritual guide, social movement leader and activist, thinker-philosopher, tantric teacher - and he was impressive in all of them," Taub wrote. "I spent several weeks at Sarkar's main ashram in Jamalpur on the Ganges, in Bihar State, where Sarkar was regularly in attendance. My purpose in being in Jamalpur was to learn tantric practice and Sarkar's social, economic, and religious ideas underpinning them. But for some reason, Mr. Sarkar's macrohistorical theory, the Proutist theory of history, was not included in my courses. I learned about it much later, in 1980, from the Australian Proutist magazine, Dharma."

Taub's caste model differs from Sarkar's theory in several ways. Sarkar refers to the Spiritual Caste as intellectuals, while Taub speaks of "seekers." Sarkar, like Marx, limits the Worker Caste to those doing manual labor, while Taub includes white-color workers and the managerial class (and the *technocrati*). Sarkar's cycle starts with the Worker Caste, followed by warriors, the intellectuals, and the merchants; Taub, like the original Hindu version, starts with the Spiritual Caste (Spiritual-Religious Age I), followed by the Warrior Caste, the Merchant Caste, and the Worker Caste, followed by a new spiritual age, his Spiritual-Religious Age 2 (see Fig. 1).

Contemporary developments suggest Taub's caste sequence is currently playing out in the world. We are currently in the Worker Caste, while the transition to Spiritual-Religious Age 2 is driven by humanity becoming dissatisfied with materialism and the Worker Age "rat race." In the near future, it will also be driven by the need to look for meaning in life when people can no longer identify with their work. Technology (smart robots, 3D printing, artificial intelligence, etc.) replaces both the need for and value of human labor. When secular and materialist values no longer satisfy, people turn to religious and spiritual alternatives.

Taub's caste sequence resonated with Futures researcher Takuya Murata, who reviewed Taub's book for *Futures Magazine* in 2007. Murata wrote: "As today is the Worker Age, in Taub's view, the Spiritual-Religious Age should follow next. By this logic, events relating to religion and spirituality should be currently emerging issues. This does seem to be happening globally in different ways. The Islamic Revolution of 1979 occurred against the secularizing trend of both Capitalism and Communism. In the 1990s, the collapse of the secular Soviet Union was followed by the return of Muslim practices to Central Asia. We are indeed seeing the emergence of religious-political groups, for instance, the Christian Right in Europe and the US and the BJP in India. Islamic Fundamentalism has become a household word post-9/11; but there are many varieties of religious Fundamentalism. Taub's prediction fits at the intersection of the global re-emergence of religion and the social search for meaning in this increasingly consumerist world."

Taub and Sarkar also have different views on the nature of the caste cycle. The original Hindu version speaks of humanity going through endless cycles. Once the four castes had their day in the sun, the cycle would start anew. Sarkar accepts the original prophecy of endless cycles, while Taub sees only one such cycle. He would argue that humanity, once in a spiritual age, would lack the need to return to a new Warrior Age. Given that the ancient sages were attuned to the universal source of Creation, their view may have gone beyond the geocentric. They spoke of *kalpas* and *yugas*, suggestive of timeframes that apply to cosmic transformation, like the implosion of solar systems and the births of new universes, where life regenerates and restarts the cycle.

Taub believed the caste cycle can help us to better understand the world as it is, enabling us to make better choices, whether on a personal level, or as policymakers or business leaders. Aside from Feminism, Taub had no ideology. His models are tools that enable us to make our own interpretations of history, understand the present, and anticipate possible future scenarios. His macrohistory is free of cultural bias or social idealism. It is as if he says: "Here are the models. Feel free to interpret them. If they further your understanding of the world or broaden your consciousness, so much the better."

Sarkar, by contract, believed the models could spur humanity into action. He believed each individual in every caste age could help the caste cycle forward. Sohail Inayatullah, a leading Sarkar scholar who was sympathetic to Taub's macrohistory, wrote a critique of Taub's book and contrasted his intentions with Sarkar. He wrote:

"The purpose for Sarkar was never to describe the world to be clever but to give resources for analysis so that the world could be changed so that cycles could be transformed, so that individually and collectively more bliss could be realized. Sarkar's theories of macrohistory, thus, I believe should be seen as new categories which expand on Marx's class. They reframe past and potential futures. I would prefer not to get lost in the 'prediction' game, rather, the purpose of macrohistory is to help us see new patterns, to frame questions and strategies, and most importantly to help create new futures."

First and foremost, Taub saw his models as a way of looking at human history through a different prism. He didn't answer one of the big mysteries about the insight of the ancient sages who conceived the Varna theory: Do caste cycles push humanity forward, or does humanity push the caste cycles forward? If humanity pushes the cycles, how does it know which cycle should be next? Taub was a seeker and he knew what he didn't know. Once, when talking about the Vedic sages who prophesized the caste cycle, he exclaimed: "How could they have known that?"

In Taub's Caste Model, we are now in the revolutionary stage of the rise to power of the new Spiritual-Religious Caste. During the first Religious-Spiritual Age, says Taub, humanity developed religion and spirituality. Having gone through the Warrior, Merchant, and Worker Caste Ages, humanity now enters a new Religious-Spiritual Age. In both the Hindu prophecy and in Taub's Caste Model, the first Religious-Spiritual Age was the age of spiritual birth, and the second, now emerging Religious-Spiritual Age 2, is the age of spiritual rebirth, the biblical equivalent to the Second Coming of Jesus.

In the 19th century, the Indian mystic Sri Yukteswar, in his book *The Holy Science*, introduced the so-called short-count yugas. Sri Yukteswar changed the order of the four caste cycle and argued that we are currently in the Merchant Age. In his cycle, the Spiritual Age lasted from 16300 to 6700 BCE, the Warrior Age from 6700 to 3100 BCE, the Merchant Age from 3100 to 700 BCE, and the *Kali Yuga* (Worker Age): from 700 BC to 1600 CE. We are now said to be in an expanded Merchant Age, 1600 to 4100 CE, to be followed by the next Warrior Age from 4100 to 7700 CE, and the next Spiritual age 7700 to 12500 CE, an age of the highest spiritual culture.

Sri Yukteswar's system is said to have been the result of his own self-realization. He based his reasoning on the correlation of inner consciousness and outward behavior. As human consciousness changes, so do civilization and human development. Taub would have agreed with the latter. But he stayed with the caste sequence of the original Vedic scriptures, and made a convincing case that we have left the Merchant Age and moved into the Worker Age.

Part 2
P.R. Sarkar and Lawrence Taub

On the differences with the related model of Sarkar
By Lawrence Taub

Aside from the Hindu philosophy of castes and ages itself, from which the Caste Model derives, two other macrohistories that resemble the Caste Model are those of Hegel and, surprisingly perhaps, Marx. Though Marx's past stages of history, on which he bases the proletariat's overthrow of capitalism, resemble the past stages of the Caste Model, his view of the future stages differs: He sees the worker caste and the Worker Age playing the key "heroic" future role, whereas the Caste Model, closer to Hegel, sees the human race climaxing in a Spiritual Age. The basic differences between the Caste Model and Marx's grand historical narrative are detailed in the book's Introduction.

What most likely will pop into your heads as resembling the Caste Model will be the macrohistory of P. R. Sarkar.

You may have read the excellent critique of The Spiritual Imperative by Takuya Murata in the May 2007 edition of Futures. [See Chapter 5, Ed.] In it, Murata notes many differences and similarities between P.R. Sarkar's macrohistory and the Caste Model. As he writes, both derive from Indian philosophy, both are based on the concept that a dominant feature characterizes each Age, and both ascribe the cause that makes one Age pass to the next to the disintegration of the age itself rather than an external force.

The key difference he notes is that, in Sarkar's model, the Ages move in a cycle that continues endlessly through human history – humans pass through many Intellectual, Warrior, and Merchant ages. That is, Sarkar's is truly a cyclical model, while the Caste Model says that human history makes up only one cycle: it's a spiral that combines a linear and cyclical element, as explained earlier

Here are a few more differences between the Sarkar and Caste Models: While both models include Warrior and Merchant Ages, Sarkar does not include a Worker Age; he sees no age in which the worker caste exercises actual power. The worker caste basically serves as a pawn for his other three castes. He therefore sees only three ages per cycle, not four, as the Caste Model does. Second, since Sarkar's model doesn't recognize a spiritual-religious caste, it doesn't include spiritual-religious ages either, as the Caste Model does. Instead, Sarkar posits an intellectual caste that rules Intellectual Ages, a caste that rules through "head knowledge" rather than through a religious, spiritual, or wisdom orientation.

The third difference, therefore, is that while the Caste Model sticks for its source to the generic, everyday, popular version of the Hindu theory of castes and ages, with four traditionally-recognized castes and ages, Sarkar developed his own unique, original version, with only three castes ruling instead of four, one of which is an intellectual rather than a spiritual-religious caste.

I was lucky enough to actually meet P.R. Sarkar, back in 1966, while in India for a two-year stay. Mr. Sarkar wore many hats – spiritual guide, social movement leader and activist, thinker-philosopher, tantric teacher – and was impressive in all of them. His followers included people of all ranks and many castes all over India, and I was privileged to be at the train station when the organization's first member to be sent abroad left for Nairobi to set up a center to make Sarkar's teachings available beyond India.

I spent several weeks at Sarkar's main ashram in Jamalpur on the Ganges, in Bihar State, where Sarkar was regularly in attendance. My purpose in being in Jamalpur was to learn tantric practice and Sarkar's social, economic, and religious ideas underpinning them.

But for some reason, Mr. Sarkar's macrohistorical theory, the Proutist theory of history, was not included in my courses. I learned about it much later, in 1980, from the Australian Proutist magazine, Dharma. That was five years after I "discovered" the three models, which derived from another Indian source.

After leaving Jamalpur I visited Varanasi (Benares). In my eagerness to soak up as much Hindu and Buddhist lore as possible, I attended a lecture at the local Brahma Kumari Center. It was from that speaker that I first heard a presentation of the traditional, generic, version of the Hindu theory of the castes and ages, with all the religious mythology and accoutrements attached.

The ideas of the lecturer didn't have much of an impact on me. As a student of history as conventionally presented, they struck me as curious nonsense, with little relation to "real" history. The only reason they stuck in my mind over the next nine years was because I often came across them in many contexts.

But one day, in 1975, in Tokyo, I read in the Japan Times how the North Vietnamese had completed their takeover of Saigon the previous day. The insight suddenly hit me: The worker caste was taking over worldwide from the merchant caste. I realized that the traditional Hindu theory of castes and ages actually contained a rough macrohistorical description of how history developed, stage-by-stage, and what the basic directions of the future were likely to be.

When I came across Sarkar's version of that idea five years later, it struck me as too divergent from the traditional version to be as valuable to me for describing history and foreseeing the future as that generic version. Though, based on my experience with macrohistorical thinking during those intervening five years, I could imagine that Sarkar's unique and original version could serve as an insight into history and the future for someone else – or myself at a later date.

Sarkar's Proutist theory overlaps – and reinforces – the Caste Model on at least two key points. First, like the Caste Model, the Proutist theory is rational-scientific rather than mythic-religious in tone. Though likewise derived from the Hindu core idea, it discards its mythic religious accouterments; it speaks to the modern-scientific Western(ized) worldview most of us, including futurists, share. Sarkar, the Indian "guru" and tantric, was also a modern Western thinker. His use of the Hindu core idea as the basis for his rational-scientific theory thus validates the Caste Model's similar use of it.

Second, though the Proutist macrohistory is basically cyclical, with history endlessly repeating itself, it has at least one feature that lets you see human history as a single, non-repetitive cycle, as the Caste Model does. That is, though Sarkar sees world power in the future reverting to the intellectual caste (the *vipra*), he says it's possible that the intellectuals who take over worldwide will be *sadvipra* (spiritually evolved intellectuals). These seem to resemble the Caste Model's future spiritual-religious caste.

The big difference is: Sarkar sees the future influence of the *sadvipra* as possible, whereas the Caste Model sees the equivalent coming Spiritual-Religious Age as almost inevitable. But this coincidence of foresight seems to put the Proutist theory and the Caste Model in the same ballpark.

***

Sarkar's Contribution to Macrohistory and Futures Imaginations

by Sohail Inayatullah

I enjoyed reading Larry TAUB'S essay *Sex, Age, and Caste: the grandest narrative of all*. I am quite sympathetic to his overall project particularly that of contextualizing trends in the broader patterns of macrohistory as well as in using theory to enlist support in creating a more gender partnership- oriented society.

I am also pleased that his work is gaining traction in Japan and elsewhere, and wish him the utmost success in his work as a futurist.

CLARIFICATIONS

I would, however, like to clarify the part of his work linked to SARKAR in general and to macrohistory in particular (1). First, I do have a problem with the construction of caste as "Hindu". A historical reading is important. The caste structure developed with the Aryan invasion of India (2). The indigenous population, who generally followed Shiva and Tantric practices, were vanquished and became the lower caste. The Aryans imposed their structure of warrior, trader and priest on the local population and made them the workers, the shudras. Overtime, this structure became solidified in Indian society. While there remain some Indian thinkers who believe it gives some necessary discipline to a chaotic society, most would assert that it is the single most violent system in the world, thus the paradox of India - a civilization that places individual non-violence as primary, yet its deeper structure is foundational and systemically violent.

This is important to raise here as SARKAR'S work was not just focused on change in individual behaviour but social behaviour as well … in the Indian context this was and continues to be the ending of caste.

Second, it is important to note that Hindu is a recent category, invented by Muslims (over a century plus ago) and now recently has gained legitimacy with the conservative right wing in India. Traditionally, as Ashis NANDY (3) has pointed out, there were endless gods and gurus vying for attraction, vying for loyalty – epistemological pluralism had been historically built into the psyche of Indian civilization. The conservative elements in Indian politics have sought to invent an institutionalized Hindu identity (one god, one people, one nation) as a wedge politics against other religions particularly Muslims. The genocide in Gujarat as Garda GHISTA (4) has written is one result of this strategy.

An alternative tack is that of seeing many eclectic traditions in Indian history, even as the overall project is similar. The overall project beginning with Tantra thousands of year ago to modernist India today remains: the understanding of the self as central; knowledge as additive not exclusionary; epistemology as pluralistic, instead of the division of wrong or right knowledge, generally a softer depth and shallow approach is taken; and inner bliss as the overall goal (eupsychia).

Third, TAUB argues that SARKAR'S four stage model is in fact a three stage model. SARKAR was very clear on this: the worker stage is a real and pivotal stage but it is short lived, not absent. Additionally, the theory of the social cycle is based on evolutionary theory informed by dynamic models of general systems theory. That is, the future to some extent remains open, humans have agency — the future is not a fixed railway. Thus, it could be as workers are more informed by the peer-to-peer revolution, as the skills revolution continues, and if we enter a post-capitalist system, the workers era may last longer. But generally, this force is more chaotic, revolutionary, seeing to redress imbalances, often and unfortunately in violent ways. After the workers era, the system undergoes a pendulum shift as the structure and order of the warrior episteme enters.

Fourth, this raises the issue of cyclicity and linearity. As Prout scholars have argued extensively elsewhere, SARKAR includes a cyclical dimension (the social cycle of the four ages, epistemes) and a linear dimension. This is his theory of evolution, which has three aspects: physical clash (or survival of the fittest, mutation), intellectual clash (memetic evolution, new ideas) and the attraction of the Great, or bliss. In this sense, bliss functions as a strange attractor guiding humanity forward. We can of course become personally and conceptually lost in the physical battle or intellectual battle but it is this move toward inner and outer bliss that brings in direction that is decisive in creating the future. Purpose is not lost in evolution. This bliss however does not – as in many religious views or via Hegel – enter the nation, it cannot be owned by any particular person or civilization. Indeed, as SARKAR has argued in his work on neo-humanism, it goes beyond humanism as well, to include plants and animals (5). And I have argued, neohumanism can and will most likely extend to include artificial intelligence as robots become more sentient (the rights of robots, if you will).

Fifth, the spiral emerges from the sadvipra. She/he is not just the pure intellectual but rather has managed to integrate and balance the different aspects of personality, i.e. knows how to serve others, can use ideas for the collective good, can use matter and ideas to create wealth and can protect others. By integrating these different paradigms of self, the sadvipra leader attempts to ensure that no one varna stays in power too long. He or she creates the appropriate transformative momentum to ensure that if the intellectuals are disowning money and the market, an economic paradigm shift is required; if the trader disowns the other, nature, gender, equity, then they bring on an social revolution. Using his or futurist and macrohistorical hat, the sadvipra leader keeps the cycle moving. This movement is not just to the next stage but it is to a synthetic advanced level wherein there is more neohumanism (i.e. less nationalism, religiousism, etc.) toward bliss – the spiral. As well, the speed of the cycles can be increased (500 years of capitalism is enough!).

And this is crucial, the future cannot be precisely or accurately predicted – the universe is open and is being co-created even though there are evolutionary derived patterns of history that structure reality. Part of the role of the sadvipra is to facilitate, to be a hand-maiden for this new possible future.

SARKAR'S FOUR EPISTEMES · PETER HAYWARD

Varna	**Focus**	**Healthy**	**Perverse**
Worker (*Shudra*)	Material needs	Service	Withdrawal and chaos
Warrior (*Ksattryia*)	Order through use of power	Protect, honour, care	Oppression, corruption
Intellectual (*Vipra*)	Power of ideas	Creative, Inspirational, Spiritual, Artistic	Dogma, Suppression, Inquisition
Merchant (*Vaeshya*)	Fulfill needs through exchange	Markets, enterprise, opportunities	Consumerism, Accumulation, Distraction, Desensitisation

Now what, as Ashis Nandy has warned us of, avoids the tyranny of the future, that is what ensures escape-ways built in to any theory of everything. These in my view are: first, the importance of spiritual practice in this endeavour …that is, seeing the social cycle not just as an external reality but as part of the inner make up. That is to say, within one's politics of the self, which varna is dominant? Is my trader self dominant (negotiating value between sub-personalities), my worker (serve other selves), my warrior (protecting my other selves or …). Second, comes from the tantric tradition – namely, what is, is not wrong or right but there are levels of reality. Third, there is no way anyone can be anointed a sadvipra …it is a bottom-up, grassroots revolution – leaders are noticed by what they do, not what they say they do! Fourth, learning comes from doing, from experimenting.

I raise the fourth as I find macrohistory not just of interest because of its broad sweep of understanding but for its utility in organizational strategy. In over a hundred workshops, I have found that organizations can use SARKAR'S work to discern which varna or episteme is dominant. What do they need to do to transform? How can violence (physical, emotional and structural) be avoided? How can they create value oriented leaders who are balanced and dynamic? Peter HAYWARD and Joe VOROS' work is instructive. They have taken macrohistory and made it organizationally relevant via the SARKAR Game. In this game, individuals in an organization play out the different varnas and then analyze the role of each varna concluding with the centrality of foresight oriented situational leadership (knowing when to play which role)(6).

PURPOSE

The purpose for SARKAR was never to describe the world to be clever but to give resources for analysis so that the world could be changed, so that cycles could be transformed, so that individually and collectively more bliss could be realized. SARKAR'S theories of macrohistory, thus, I believe should be seen as new categories which expand on MARX'S class. They reframe past and potential futures. I would prefer not to get lost in the "prediction" game; rather, the purpose of macrohistory is to help us see new patterns, to frame questions and strategies, and most importantly to help create new futures. Within the predictive game, I find using many macrohistorians in an eclectic way can be quite powerful for scenario generation (i.e. the pendulum of SOROKIN with the linearity of SMITH with the spiral of SARKAR, for example). That said, there are a good number of books, particularly by Ravi BATRA, which use SARKAR to make bold forecasts (7). The most important aspect of these contributions is to use foresight to avoid certain default futures and instead choose more balanced blissful pathways. Accuracy of prediction does not prove a theory as other factors could explain correlation, including luck. Finally, theories themselves exist at different levels – macro (broad, through space and time), meso (organizational) and micro (day to day understandings).

As to TAUB'S last point the determined future, I am not sure if SARKAR believed a society of sadvipras was inevitable, but he remained positive all along foreseeing a world where communism, capitalism and religiousism would disappear. This foreseeing was based on understanding the factors of history but also on inspiring others to invent and create an alternative future. Inevitability as strategy is intelligible, inevitability as theory is hazardous since structure will then reign over agency.

Futures Studies, as I see it, even while understanding structure (patterns of macrohistory, trends, inner frameworks) transforms us by making agency attractive, not by giving hope (8) but by pointing us toward possibility, which then can become reality.

Sohail INAYATULLAH is a Professor, Tamkang University, Adjunct Professor,

University of the Sunshine Coast, Associate, prout college. www.proutcollege.org, www.metafuture.org.I do this in the context of having authored two books on Sarkar (Understanding Sarkar: the indian episteme, macrohistory and transformative knowledge. Brill, Leiden, 2002; Situating Sarkar: tantra, macrohistory and alternative futures. Maleny, Gurukul, 1999) and edited two books on Sarkar/macrohistory (Macrohistory and Macrohistorians. Westport, Praeger, 1987, with Johan Galtung; Transcending Boundaries: Prabhat Rainjan Sarkar's Theories of Individual and Social Transformation. Maleny, Gurukul, 1999 with Jennifer Fitzgerald) as well articles in Futures, the Routlege Encyclopedia of Indian Philosophy, Development etc on Sarkar and his social movement, Prout. For more on prout, see,
www.proutcollege.org,
www.proutinstitute.org
www.priven.org/
www.worldproutassembly.org/

(1) See Romila Thapar, A History of India. Baltimore, Penguin Books, 1966. See Rajni Kothari, Caste in Indian Politics. New Delhi, Orient Longman, 1970.

(2) Ashis Nandy, Traditions, Tyrannys and Utopias.

Delhi, Oxford University Press, 1987.

(3) Garda Ghista, The Gujarat Genocide. Bloomington, Indiana, Authorhouse, 2006.

(4) See Sohail Inayatullah, Marcus Bussey and Ivana Milojevic, eds., Neohumanist Educational Futures. Tamsui, Tamkang University, 2006.

(5) See Peter Hayward and Joesph Voros, "Playing the neohumanist game, " in Neohumanist Educational Futures: Liberating the pedagogical intellect. Tamsui, Tamkang University, 2006, pages, 283-296.

(6) See Ravi Batra, Muslim Civilization the Crisis in Iran. Dallas, Venus Books, 1980. Ravi Batra, The Downfall of Capitalism and Communism. London, Macmillan, 1978. Ravi Batra, The Great Depression of 1990. New York,
Bantam, 1988. Ravi Batra, The New Golden Age. London, Palgrave Macmillan, 2007. www.ravibatra.com

(7) As John Cleese tells it in the movie Clockwork: Despair I can handle, it is hope I can't stand.

Part 3
P2P Foundation Interview

(Q) Of the three models you use, the Caste Model seems the most prominent. How can an ancient Indian social system be useful to a futurist?

(A) The Caste Model is derived from the Hindu caste philosophy first referred to in the Rig Veda. It recognizes four main castes: the religious or spiritual caste; the warrior caste; the merchant caste; and the worker caste. The Indians believe that each caste rules the world in turn. In other words, the world goes through a Religious-Spiritual Caste Age, followed by a Warrior Age, then a Merchant Age, then a Worker Age, and then back to a second Spiritual-Religious Age to start a new cycle. The notion of caste is generally misunderstood. We have to see the different castes as generic types.

(Q) Generic types?

(A) Yes, in the sense that every person has features of all four castes, but those of one caste dominate. The people within each caste share that caste's world view, value system, and

social ideal. According to my model, derived from this Hindu idea, the world view of the religious-spiritual caste is based on God, spiritual freedom, and Enlightenment. That of the warrior caste revolves around war and physical competition. The merchant caste values money and material possessions, and the worker caste is all about identification with work, skill, and job. My model says that we are now in a transition from the Merchant Age, which has just about ended, to the peak point of the Worker Age. We live in an age of identification with work. One of the first questions people ask each other is "What do you do?," which means "What kind of work do you do?" In Japan people ask, "What company do you belong to?" Up to the 19th century, it was not your job but your family name that counted, and after that how much money you had.

(Q) *How does your Caste Model differ from the Indian prototype?*

(A) The Hindus understood the Religious/Spiritual-Warrior-Merchant-Worker sequence to be cyclical. When completed, it starts anew and repeats itself indefinitely. My Caste Model adds a linear, historical time-line, so that the ages run in a spiral rather than a

cycle. In other words, I matched up the different caste ages with the different periods of prehistory and history that we're familiar with, plus the future. Secondly, I added a geographical dimension. To give an example, the world power of 16th century Spain and Portugal marked the peak stage of the Warrior Age. The first world power of the Merchant Age was the 17th century Dutch Republic, after it cast off the Spanish yoke. America's world power represents the peak of the Merchant Age. In other words, different countries or cultures show the characteristics of one or another caste. Countries rise when the caste they belong to rises during its age, and fall as the next caste rises to replace it. So the Model actually clarifies why different world powers and empires rose and fell in the past and which countries or regions can be expected to become powerful in the future. The Indian prototype, of course, lacks these historical and geographical elements.

(Q) America's world power represents the peak of the Merchant Caste Age. You mean we are now moving to the Worker Caste Age?

(A) That's right. But the Worker Age has its roots in the 19th century. That's when the blue-collar segment of the worker caste organized to resist its oppressor, the merchant caste power elite. It was the time of the utopian socialists, the anarchist and communist movements and the first trade unions. Then came the worker-caste, socialist-communist revolutions that started in 1917. The Worker Age is now starting to peak in the Far East. The people of that region best match the psychological profile of the worker caste. The Japanese, Chinese and Koreans best identify with the value system, social organization and world view of the worker caste.

(Q) *The transitions of power from one caste to the next overlap?*

(A) Yes. The peak of the Worker Age is now starting. But the beginning, pioneering stage of the new religious-spiritual caste's rise to power is already over. It lasted from the 1950s to the 1970s, and was characterized by two opposite religious and spiritual tendencies. One was the counterculture, the beatniks, the hippies, the human potential movement, transpersonal theory, the environmental, and especially the feminist movements. The other was the mass return to religious orthodoxy. Examples are born-again Christians, fundamentalist Moslems, and baal-teshuvah Jews. The next, revolutionary stage of the new caste's rise to power is already underway. It began with the Islamic Revolution in Iran, and continues with the fundamentalist takeover of Afghanistan.

(Q) *The rise of each caste to world rule happens in stages? How does it work?*

(A) I distinguish three stages: the pioneering stage, the revolutionary-evolutionary stage and the peak stage. In the pioneering stage, the rising caste organizes and sets up pockets of power and opposition to the ruling caste. This usually happens in the main centers of world power, where the ruling caste is most powerful and from where it rules the rest of the world. In the second stage, the rising caste takes power mainly through revolution in some undeveloped countries. Take the worker caste revolutions. They happened in Russia, Yugoslavia, Mongolia, China, North Korea, Vietnam, Cuba and Nicaragua, away from the main centers of merchant caste power in North America, Western Europe and Japan. But the revolutions help the rising caste gain power even in those main centers. That happens in a more evolutionary rather than revolutionary way, which is why I call this second stage the revolutionary-evolutionary stage. I mark 1917 as the beginning of the revolutionary-evolutionary stage of the Worker Age, and 1979 as the end. Those were the years of the Russian and Nicaraguan revolutions respectively. The third and last stage of a caste's rise to world rule is the peak stage. That's when the caste reaches the height of its power and rules the world, but also ripens itself for falling. This stage unfolds in those countries that have evolved to be most in tune with the spirit and world view of the rising caste. The peak stage of the Warrior Age unfolded in the Spanish, Portuguese and Ottoman Empires and Ming China. The Merchant Age's peak stage is today's United States. The Worker Age's peak stage will unfold in what I call the Confucian bloc, over the next 30-40 years. That bloc will consist of China, Japan, and Korea. It may seem far-fetched, but I foresee the peak stage of Religious-Spiritual Age No. 2 in sub-Saharan Africa, but that's at least a century ahead.

(Q) Some of what you just said sounds like a theory of revolution. Is that also what the Caste Model provides?

(A) Pretty much so. It shows that revolutions are inevitable in human history. Marx and the Marxists had it a little wrong. History does not progress through class struggle, as they thought, but on the much deeper level of caste

struggle. The ancient Hindus understood this principle. And caste struggle includes revolution, by its very nature destructive and fundamentalistic.

(Q) *You argue that the four castes each have their own class structure. Can you explain?*

(A) Think of each caste as a pyramid. In the Merchant Age now drawing to a close, the top of the merchant caste pyramid was occupied by the grand bourgeoisie of the wealthiest entrepreneurs, capitalists, industrialists, landlords and financiers. In the middle were the smaller entrepreneurs, traders, factory owners, landlords and financial people, and at the bottom were the hordes of small shopkeepers and traders, the 'petty bourgeoisie'. In the present Worker Age, the top of the worker-caste pyramid is occupied by the bureau-technostructure: the top executives of the big corporations, the top sci-technicians, professionals, government, party and labor leaders. In the middle level you have the less-powerful people of the same type. At the bottom are the 'wage slaves' - the armies of white- and blue-collar and agricultural workers, housewives, the unemployed and the homeless.

(Q) The Indian caste philosophy sees the caste ages as a regression. The Religious-Spiritual Age is like heaven, the Warrior Age not so good, the Merchant Age quite bad, and the Worker Age is sheer hell, reflecting the progressively lower quality of the castes themselves. Do you agree?

(A) Yes and no. I synthesize the regressive Indian view and the progressive Western view. In some ways the ages regress, but there's no denying that each successive caste age advanced human consciousness. The Warrior Age was brutal and imperialistic, and kept the human race continually at war. But conquests by warrior kings like Constantine and Ashoka spread advanced spiritual consciousness through Christianity and Buddhism. The Warrior Age also introduced such concepts as individual freedom and personal salvation, and a sense of moral and ethical responsibility. The Merchant Age raised the level of material well-being for masses of people, launched the Industrial Revolution, ended slavery, and introduced the modern concept of democracy for all. The present Worker Age was the first age to reject war and imperialism. It embraced sexual, racial and ethnic equality, and developed class consciousness and worker-caste solidarity. The worker caste was also the

first to demand the right for all to basic human needs such as food, shelter, education, and medical care. Looked at in this way, it can't be denied that each caste contributed to human spiritual and material development.

(Q) We are now in the Worker Age but we have already witnessed the advent of the next, Religious-Spiritual Age No. 2. Can you explain?

(A) The revolutionary-evolutionary stage of the Religious-Spiritual Age has already started with the religious revolutions in Iran and Afghanistan. These two countries are part of what I call the religious belt, which stretches from Bangladesh and Tibet across India, Pakistan, Afghanistan, Iran, Central Asia, Turkey, Kurdistan, the Arab-Israeli Middle East to North Africa. More revolutions are likely to occur in this region. And they will all be religious revolutions, as in Iran and Afghanistan, not socialist ones. This is because the revolutionaries, like the Taliban, are religious caste, not worker caste.

(Q) When you say religious revolutions, do you mean fundamentalist revolutions?

(A) Yes, but the revolutions won't stay fundamentalist. This has to do with the dynamics of caste revolution in general. Take the French and Russian revolutions, of the Merchant and Worker Ages respectively. They too started out with fundamentalists in control, who organized reigns of terror. But fundamentalism is impractical in the long run. Sooner or later the terror dies down. Pragmatists come into power who either replace or purge the fundamentalist generation. The religious revolutions of the religious belt will probably follow this pattern, as we already see in Iran. As the terror dies down, these countries will move away from fundamentalism and other doctrinaire forms of religiosity. They will move toward a more enlightened spirituality.

(Q) How will that come about?

(A) The Sex Model, one of the three macrohistories in my book, suggests that women in the religious belt will play the leading role in taking these countries from fundamentalism to spirituality. Looking at Afghanistan today, this idea may seem far-fetched, especially when viewed from our present vantage point in the middle of the Worker Age. But we have clear indications that women will exert the main influence in the religious belt. This region has already seen

more women prime ministers than any other region in the world. I should also point out the role of feminism, which has resulted in a growing influence of women in religions everywhere. This trend will spread to the religious belt, where religious power will translate into political power. The growing influence of women in religion will decrease the power of the male fundamentalist ruling elites. The two cannot co-exist.

(Q) Is this what the Sex Model tells us?

(A) The Sex Model holds that humanity evolves according to a sexual dialectic, from the female principle to the male principle to the androgynous. As a metaphor I use the ancient Chinese concepts of Yin and Yang. The Sex Model holds that humanity first experienced a Yin Age, the prehistoric period, followed by a Yang Age, which began with the Patriarchal Revolution between 2000 and 4000 BC. We are now in the transition from the Yang to the Androgynous Age. The beginning of this latter age was marked by the feminist movement that began in the sixties. Our new holistic outlook, the environmental and gay movements, and many other new trends are indicative of the androgynous direction we are heading in. As androgynization proceeds, everything that was either too yin or too yang in the Yang Age will become sexually balanced. The Sex Model makes forecasts related to the environment, medicine, animal rights, the bisexual nature of future religion, homosexuality, hunting and cruel sports, the role of women in politics, business and society, and what male-female love-sex relationships will be like as we become more androgynous.

(Q) *Your Sex Model argues that the West is essentially yang and the East essentially yin. Can you explain?*

(A) At the dawn of history, the start of the Yang Age, the world split culturally into East and West. The yang world view developed more strongly in the West than in the East, reaching its peak with the Western development of science and technology. This split is reflected in the main world religions. The Eastern world religions - Hinduism and Buddhism - are primarily yin, while the three monotheistic religions of the West - Judaism, Christianity, and Islam - are essentially yang. Jerusalem, the focal city of Western religion, became humanity's yang-male pole, while Varanasi [Benares], the focal city of the Eastern world religions, became its yin-female pole. Both Eastern and Western culture became more yang during the Yang Age. But the East stayed closer to humanity's prehistoric yin-origins, and didn't become yang enough, while Western culture suppressed most of its prehistoric female roots and became too yang. Androgynization also means we will integrate Eastern and Western culture, philosophy, religion, and sensibility. I believe the Sex Model connection is the clincher.

Part 4
Lawrence Taub: Life and Work
Bill Kelly

Larry Taub's life is worth reflecting on because he was a gifted and creative theorist of history. I want to celebrate his achievement and to take a look at his theory and predictions today, many years after he came up with them. I will also give a brief rundown of Taub's relation with his times and explore the connection between his life and values besides focusing on his work. It is revealing to see how the ideologies that influenced him pushed his work in certain directions.

A Prophetic Gift

I became close friends with Taub in Tokyo at the start of the 1980s, and we remained close until I left Japan in 1996. The 1980s were the time when Taub was writing *The Spiritual Imperative,* and he often discussed his ideas with me. His predictions really got my attention. Just a few of the most arresting ones were that Japan, China, and a reunified Korea would form a cultural and economic bloc headed by China while becoming the next center of the world, a new spiritual era would follow the relatively brief period when East Asian nations occupied world leadership, the current age of patriarchy would give way to an androgynous age, and women would be at the forefront of the spiritual revolution that would be led by India, the Islamic world, and Israel.

There were several other bold and fairly concrete predictions about the shape of the world to come. Since nobody at that time was making such predictions, I was very interested in finding out how he could penetrate the future. I was also intrigued by his theory. Popular writers were coming up with stage theories of history, for example, Alvin Toffler in *The Third Wave* (1980), in which he described three waves, the agricultural, industrial, and postindustrial (information) eras. But Taub used three models based on caste, sex, and age, not just one like Toffler, whose economic approach resembles Taub's caste model.

I asked Taub how he was able to make his far-reaching predictions. What was his special gift? He gave two types of answers. One was that the predictions came from the theory; the other was that his ability was part intuitive and part analysis and anyone could develop these abilities. But he never gave me a satisfying response to my question as to why very few people had developed such abilities. Was it simply a matter of people not developing that ability because the dominant view was that such abilities do not exist? Or did his experience of living in many parts of the world and his life as a free-floating intellectual uniquely qualify him?

The Three Models Revisited

Many years later, it is easier to evaluate the quality of his theory and the acuity of his predictive skills. His theory of the four castes is unexceptional in the sense that many have offered stage theories in economic terms. Although Taub talks about castes, it is quite simple to translate caste into class. If we take his idea that a worker caste succeeds the merchant caste and we define worker to include knowledge workers, bureaucrats, and managers, then his theory dovetails with standard accounts of a shift from an entrepreneur-based economy to one centered around the managerial class.

More provocative, though, is his prediction that a new spiritual era will succeed the worker caste age we are now entering. This means that motivation for action will change from satisfying survival needs to our highest aspiration, to uncover who we really are. Here his predecessors were Aurobindo, Teilhard, de Chardin, Jean Gebser, and Ken Wilber. He had read Aurobindo but not the others. He was always reluctant to acknowledge predecessors so I didn't ask him whether Aurobindo's work on the human cycle had influenced him. But he did refer to Aurobindo's distinction between religion and spirituality, which appears in his own theory as a key difference between the first spiritual era (religion) and the coming spiritual era. On my recommendation, he read Wilber's *Up from Eden* (1981) which he enjoyed, finding Wilber's ideas about the evolution of consciousness compatible with his own.

There are clear signs that a transition toward a new spiritual era has begun. For example, the World Values Survey has identified the presence of postmaterialist values in industrial societies. Taub also viewed the Iranian Revolution of 1979 as the first major event heralding the new spiritual age. But a shift away from a warrior-age mentality to a truly spiritual rather than conventionally religious outlook is still in its early stages. Among many Islamists there is support for elections, the rule of law, and the separation of power, the indicators of a liberal (merchant) standpoint. But Sufism, which emphasizes the inner awakening above all, has yet to have a large effect. Nevertheless, the high education levels of women in Iran coupled with the recent protests show that a more expansive consciousness can arise among women in the Muslim world.

The main argument in Taub's favor for believing that the spiritual revolution will be led by India, the Islamic world, and Israel is that religion is strongest in these areas. In addition, at the intellectual level, the way is already being prepared for women's leadership in a new era, since Islamic feminism has taken root and women in India are raising their consciousness in the face of male violence and extreme patriarchal attitudes. In both India and the Islamic world, what the West calls "fundamentalism" is bringing into being its opposite: women's desire for freedom and to have a greater say over their own lives and that of the society in which they live.

Taub's sex model appears to be accurate, despite the current phase of reaction in the West against increased gender flexibility and fluidity. There is a move toward androgynous ways of being, catalyzed by the realization that the masculine or yang orientation of domination over nature is leading humanity to ecological destruction. So far, though, in the West, especially the United States, the emphasis has been more on women adopting yang attitudes and going up the ladder in the corporate world and government than on promoting yin ways of thinking and feeling.

In terms of the age model, the development of consciousness is the best way to interpret it. Without a rather quick acceleration of the level of consciousness, humanity may be overwhelmed by the increasing rates of change and technological development. Such a development would allow humanity to gain control over such development rather than having it function almost autonomously or by the will of a small economic and technical elite motivated by the will to power and the desire for profit. Taub was joined by feminists who argued that conditions are ripe for a significant advance in the level of consciousness led by women. But at that time such insights among male thinkers were relatively rare with the notable exception of Fritjof Capra in *The Turning Point* (1982).

Taub's achievement, as I see it, is to bring together economics, gender, and matters of the spirit in one package. Usually, historians who focus on the material dimension ignore the spiritual realm and the reverse is also true. Those whose major concern is gender relations do not often give proper acknowledgement to both hard-core economic issues and the sphere of consciousness. Of course, Taub's combination of the three models of caste, sex, and age adds to complexity and can become difficult to apply to real-world situations but he does remarkably well in this regard, since his models cohere fairly well and his predictions enable him to achieve concreteness and specificity.

How Have Taub's Predictions Turned Out?

I would say that Taub's record as a prophet is far better than most. It is particularly impressive because the predictions were audacious and few people expected them to come true. China has gained great power, economic and military, while taking the lead among the BRICS+ nations, and he predicted this when China was very poor and just starting to recover from the chaos of the Cultural Revolution. On the other hand, in recent years, China and Japan have moved farther apart rather than formed an alliance based on economic complementarity and cultural affinities. Since the United States and Russia are at odds with each other as the war in Ukraine rages, Taub's prediction that they would come together to offset the power of the East Asian and European blocs does not seem likely. Instead, China and Russia have found a common interest in offsetting US and European power.

On a different front, the European Union came together impressively for a few decades but the momentum has slackened and the withdrawal of the United Kingdom is a setback. Taub's three major cultural-economic blocs are only partially visible. It is also not clear that a Chinese-led East Asian bloc will gain hegemony as the power of the US recedes. And Taub's prediction that the US and Europe will form separate power blocs isn't happening as they emphasize their common liberal values and attempt to get the rest of the world to follow them. The current unity over the Ukraine war is a sign of an Atlantic coalition led by the United States.

Taub believed that Israel would participate in a pan-Semitic union that would be part of the religious belt along with India and the Islamic world. But the war between Israel and Hamas is making such a union ever more difficult to achieve. Jewish and Islamic spirituality have continued to lag behind Jewish and Islamic fundamentalism, which serve as outlets for popular frustration in that part of the world. In Israel, the peace movement completely dried up, and in the Arab world, the promise of the Arab spring was dashed, except for Tunisia.

What Taub did foresee around 1980 in addition to the rise of China was the increasing strength of a religious outlook in the Islamic world, India, and Israel, a moving away from materialism among the middle-classes who can meet their basic needs, the increasing cultural and political voice of women in non-Western parts of the world, and the coming into eventual leadership in the second spiritual-religious age of indigenous peoples across the world, especially in Africa.

This last prediction at the time seemed very unlikely to be realized. But now many more people would agree that he got it right. Today there is a wave of indigenous thinkers and artists who are showing both the need for such a lifestyle and the ability of their heritage to fulfill this need; for example, the native Australian writer Tyson Yunkaporta, author of *Sand Talk: How Indigenous Thinking Can Save the World* (2020), and Lyla June Johnston, a Navajo musician, poet, scholar, and activist who has written in great detail about the concrete ways in which native knowledge and practices can contribute to a sustainable future.

Taub saw this development coming although his emphasis was different. He thought Africa, in particular, would rise because its people recognized the importance of our physicality and our bodies. Therefore, postmaterialists in the more technologically advanced regions would acknowledge African preeminence in this realm and look to it for guidance. His unique historical insight was that the outlook of the religious belt is flawed. Its anti-body and otherworldly orientation has to give way to indigenous peoples who have preserved a positive relationship with the physical world.

But his understanding of the severity of the ecological crisis was limited so he did not sufficiently appreciate just how much indigenous peoples could contribute. Not only is there a pressing need to return to the body but, even more, an imperative to make ecological thinking central in a society where spirituality includes accepting that we are part of nature, not in flight from it.

My sense is that his predictions have only been partially realized because his conception of history is too schematic, almost deterministic, leaving not enough room for the emergence of new historical trends. There are unanticipated events and developments that even the best planners can't anticipate. How many writers or leaders foresaw the ecological crisis before the 1960s? Very few.

Taub also gives too little importance to historical contingencies such as the decisions of powerful leaders. Relations among nations are not fully predictable on the basis of the struggle for hegemony alone. For one thing, national leaders make choices: Xi Jinping did not attempt to get closer to Japan when the opportunity presented itself at the beginning of his rule and US leaders provoked Russia to go to war with Ukraine by attempting to extend NATO to Russia's borders.

The Struggle for Acceptance

The translation of Taub's *The Spiritual Imperative* into Japanese sold very well when it came out, unlike the two editions of the English-language original which were self-published. The Korean translation also did fairly well. It is hardly surprising that his book was so much more popular in the region of the world whose continued rise he predicted than in the United States and Europe, whose future loss of centrality in the world he also foresaw. He appealed to the nationalism of countries that had long resented American arrogance, although they felt powerless to move out from under American protection.

When Taub's book appeared, it did not fit well with the prevailing climate of ideas in the United States and Europe. Part of the problem was that Taub was several decades ahead of most Western people in his ability to envision the world as no longer revolving around the West. What had long been the periphery was starting to take center stage, and while living in Japan in the 1970s, he saw much evidence around him to indicate the direction in which world history was moving.

Significantly, he was open to recognizing such evidence, whereas many Western people were unwilling or unable to do so because of the magnitude of the mental shift required. When it became clear that Japan was rising and that the centrality of the West might not last forever, the first impulse was often either to dismiss the idea or get carried away by a superficial enthusiasm for all things Japanese. Taub was different because he could see the implications of Japan's rise for world historical development and its relation to larger historical trends such as the coming economic ascendance of East Asia.

Taub was out of step with the time intellectually. Since he came from a working-class background and his father was a socialist, he was receptive to Marxism in its 1950s American version. Then he went to France in the late 1950s and experienced European Marxism which was the dominant political outlook among the intellectuals. His brief but passionate involvement in American feminist circles at the end of the 1960s included a close friendship with Shulamith Firestone, author of *The Dialectic of Sex*. These engagements with progressive ideas left him with an abiding confidence that thought is up to the task of mapping out the world. As a result, the increasingly skeptical orientation of postmodern philosophy had no effect on him; he simply ignored it. So his interest in coming up with a big-picture account of historical development and the future never wavered.

During a two-year stay in India in the 1960s, Taub became interested in Indian philosophy and his view of the world slowly began to shift toward a more spiritual perspective. He also encountered P.R. Sarkar, a relatively rare example of an Indian spiritual teacher who was also socially and politically engaged. Taub claimed that he went to Sarkar's ashram to learn tantric practices and did not study Sarkar's progressive utilization theory during his stay. Unlike many Western enthusiasts for

Indian philosophy, he did not give up his curiosity and fascination with the course of events in the world outside him. But his spiritually-based understanding of history left him a rather isolated figure who fit in neither with the declining left movements, the increasingly skeptical intellectuals, or the dreamy mystics floating far above the world.

The 1980s and 1990s were also a time when many Western people were more engaged in conventional lifestyles and pursuing material success than in thinking out of the box or creating visions. The longer Taub lived the expatriate life, the more out of touch he became with the typical concerns of people back home. He remained the kind of maverick you could find in the West during the late 1960s and early 1970s when more people were moving to their own inner beat. But by the 1980s most of them had made their peace with the establishment and discovered careers and family, a path that Taub never took. His unique location outside the structures of power and influence helped his creativity while making it more difficult for him to find communities that could have given his ideas a hearing.

Taub's outsider status helps us understand some important facets of his thinking. Since he never got entangled with the powers that be, he had no stake in the status quo and could take an independent position on whatever issue was at hand. This is not to say that he had no emotional stake in any of the issues that he was dealing with. Identification with the underdog was the foundation of Taub's ideological impulses and political enthusiasms during the first half of his life. But his strongest emotional bond with the underdog was with the Jewish people, which is not surprising since he was born into a working-class Jewish family in New Jersey in 1936. To a degree, he was a Jewish intellectual, although his love of conversation and socializing never left him sufficient time to really pursue that path.

He saw the poor as the underdog before discovering the depth of women's oppression as the second wave of feminism began gaining strength in the United States at the end of the 1960s. These interests led to activism in the late 1970s and early 1980s in Japan, where he energetically promoted feminist causes while maintaining a radical left outlook. For a long time after that, however, his ideological passions were no longer expressed through activism. It was only when he settled in Israel during the last years of his life that his activist inclinations returned; only this time, his orientation was rightwing.

Ideological Influences

In the late 1970s, Taub and the American scholar and translator Chris Drake wrote *Multinational Sex* under the pen names of Carl Cronstadt and Eli Tov. The theme of *Multinational Sex* was largely about the structure of economic exploitation of South Korean sex workers. They traced the historical roots of sex tourism and analyzed its contemporary manifestations as group sex tourism organized by companies and large travel agencies. Taub and Drake submitted it to South End Press, a radical left publishing house, where it was narrowly turned down by the board that ran the organization. It was then privately published and distributed.

Drake and Taub pictured a hierarchical world order with three tiers: the top-tier in which the United States was dominant and Europe held up the rear, the middle tier that Japan occupied, and the lower tier made up of what were then called Third World nations, including South Korea. There was a transfer of oppression going on whereby the United States continued to exercise its domination of Japan, while Japan economically exploited Southeast Asia and South Korea.

Taub's awareness of the purely economic side of the relationship between Japan and Southeast Asia led him to find much significance in the 1974 protests against Japan in first Thailand and then Indonesia. When he turned his gaze on the domestic United States, he made an important connection between the world economic hierarchy and the economic one in the United States. In his view, which he asserted often and with great conviction, American Jews occupied the second tier below the whites and above the blacks. In this regard, they functioned in the same way within the American hierarchy as Japanese did within the world hierarchy.

Taub used the expression "surrogate oppressor" to characterize the function of both the Jews and the Japanese in this system. In the case of the Jews, they were the middlemen in the black ghettos, the shopkeepers, the landlords, and the most visible occupying presence. They were doing white people's dirty work for them by keeping the system in place, just as the Japanese were doing the dirty work of the United States in Southeast Asia. So black people vented their rage against Jews in the same way as Southeast Asians vented their rage against the Japanese. In both cases these scapegoats deflected whatever anger might have been expressed against the real oppressors, those who set up and maintained the prevailing system for their own advantage. Many people were not aware that Jews were mostly middlemen in the United States, so it was important for Taub to demonstrate that Jews did not control the large corporations and banks and were not heavily represented within the political leadership class.

Actively involved in Japanese feminist circles in Tokyo at this time, Taub put out a few works about Japanese feminism in English through Femintern Press, the small publishing outfit that he and his girlfriend Sawako Takagi had set up. He also formed a group of male feminists that was conducted in English with both Japanese and Western members in order to explore the harmful effects of narrow gender roles on men.

Taub's feelings about Japan at least during the early 1980s were quite mixed. On the one hand, he took what might be considered the extreme position that the Japanese government made it illegal for women to use birth control because it wanted poor women to have more children. Since wealthier women get abortions, it was mainly poor women that were affected by this policy. He said the government's thinking was that if poor women had more children, then these disadvantaged and underprivileged kids could be used as cannon fodder for the Japanese military when Japan rearmed. This was part of his strong feminist stance.

On the other hand, as the trade friction with the United States heated up, he asserted that the reason for the trade deficit was not that Japan was an unfair trader. He believed that no matter what actions Japan took to satisfy US demands, the trade deficit would not go down very much. The real cause was the inefficiency of the American political economy when compared to that of Japan.

Based on the political views that Taub expressed during the early 1980s, we can identify three ideologies at work. The first is Marxism, which focused his attention on economic oppression and influenced his three-tiered view of the world hierarchy under capitalism. The second is feminism. His concern was for poor women in Japan who had no access to birth control and found it difficult to get abortions. He was equally concerned about the poor women of Southeast Asia who had to submit to indignities at the hands of Japanese male tourists in order to put food on the table for their families.

The third ideology is Zionism. As a Jewish American, Taub was very sensitive to the dangers of anti-Semitism, both past and present. He had lived in Israel and worked on a kibbutz for a while in the 1960s and spoke some Hebrew. In addition, he was well-versed in the ideas of Herzl and sympathized with the need of Jews all over the world to have a safe place of refuge in order to escape persecution.

Taub often explained how the Jews of medieval Europe could not own land so they were forced into occupations dealing with money, becoming moneylenders because the Catholic religion forbade lending money with interest payments. Jews were scapegoated as people who were obsessed with money but merchant and trade activities were the only ones open to them due to widespread discrimination. He also emphasized that whenever there are economic problems and people experience frustration due to a worsening of their financial situation, anti-Semitism always increases. It was like a social law because such scapegoating never fails to occur when economic downturns take place.

Over time, Taub began to talk less about current political affairs and more about his big picture vision of historical change. His mind was preoccupied with figuring out the likely configurations of future alliances and power blocs rather than in thinking about present-day injustices against the wretched of the earth, women, and Jews.

There was one other important reason for Taub's shift away from leftwing politics: the increasing criticism of Israel for its treatment of Palestinians by the left. This led to an ideological split with Drake who found it incomprehensible that Taub could be on the side of Israel in its conflict with the Palestinians. Drake was particularly upset by the declaration that Taub often made to the effect that one's ethnic identity came before anything else. By this he seemed to mean that it was necessary to support one's ethnic group regardless of whether or not it had justice on its side.

Zionism Takes Center Stage

How did this tangle of ideological impulses that Taub was experiencing find expression in his writing of *The Spiritual Imperative*? There is a fascinating chapter filled with commentary called "The Great 21st-Century Exodus." It follows Taub's discussion of the Pan-Semitic Federation that he expected to come into being as the last materialist age exhausted itself. The

Pan-Semitic Federation would be made up of Israel and its Arab neighbors, and, in the new spiritual-religious age, it would lead to a greater Middle-Eastern Federation, including India, more powerful than the northern cultural-economic blocs that will dominate the world during the first half of the present century. By then, spiritual riches would be the main source of power and influence.

The importance that Taub personally attached to Israel was directly echoed in his elaborate explanations of how American Jews would be motivated to emigrate to Israel and the ways in which Israel's politics would be affected by this migration. The relevance of developments in Israel for world history was that the Israeli-Palestinian conflict could lead to larger wars and even superpower involvement. But it seems that the prospect of Islamic revolutions following the one in Iran has turned out to be at least as important as developments in Israel. Yet, there is almost no analysis of the explosive social and political situations in countries like Algeria, Egypt, Iraq, and Pakistan. Events and trends in the Islamic world from Morocco to Indonesia are sketchily presented, even though together with India, these are the countries that would play the greatest part in ushering in the new spiritual-religious age.

In the chapter which highlights the exodus of Jews from the United States and their settling in Israel, he talks about the likelihood of a crusade against the Jews on the part of both blacks and whites that will be one of the main factors leading to this exodus. Once again, he relies on the notion that American blacks will express their frustration against Jews, the lightning rod, to deflect the discontent of the people below from those actually responsible for their condition. But I wonder if the Jews will continue to play this role to the extent that they did in earlier times. After all, in the 1990s, the upheavals in Los Angeles targeted the Korean shopkeepers, the new middlemen, who had replaced the Jews in the black ghettos. These days, although anti-Semitism has resurfaced among white people on the left, in particular, due to Israel's bombing Gaza, it doesn't seem as powerful or significant as anti-immigrant sentiment.

I agree, however, with Taub that it is not unthinkable that Jews could once again be persecuted in the United States. In this regard, European history does offer us reason for caution. From the late 18th century onward, Jews were increasingly integrated into

European society, but such progress was abruptly halted during the 1920s in the aftermath of World War I, especially in Germany, as racialist doctrines took hold.

In the last part of his book, Taub does not cover the status of women in any depth. He writes about the new spiritual-religious age, the religious belt, spiritualizing the economy, the ways in which a spiritual economy will make the religious belt more powerful, and finally the role of Africa and indigenous people in enabling spiritual development to reach its highest potential. This lack of attention to the role of women in bringing about crucial historical developments than usher in the new spiritual age perhaps reflects a flagging of his earlier enthusiasm for feminism. Although Islamic feminism was making headway in directions that Taub had predicted, he wrote nothing about such developments in the second edition of his book which appeared in 2002.

Taub's Zionism clearly had far more staying power than the Marxism and feminism which were so prominent in the first part of his adult life. Not only did he neglect writing about women, but his discussions of struggles between social classes are about the elites; the suffering of those at the bottom is never described except very briefly in the most abstract terms.

The Right Place at the Right Time

Looking back on Taub's long life, what stands out is his ability to be in the right place at the right time for understanding world trends. He grew up at a time when his native country was maximizing its political power in the world and asserting its economic and cultural dominance. Although the United States was in its full glory in the late 1950s, he decided to leave and go to Europe. There he encountered societies clearly divided on the basis of class. While living in France, he observed a segmented society with a clear ruling elite and well-defined working-class communities with their own culture that reliably voted communist. Unlike his home country, the existence of class boundaries was right out in the open, acknowledged by most, and unambiguously reflected in voting patterns.

Later, when he moved to Sweden, he directly experienced that social democracy produces a far more equal and humane society than laissez-faire capitalism. So his time in Europe demonstrated to him that a socialist economy made some sense. By giving prominence to class struggle and the need for government intervention to reduce the inequalities that capitalism inevitably produced, Marxism had some great advantages over the classical liberalism that was dominant in the United States. He also acquired the insight that in terms of maturity, Europe had already reached young adulthood, whereas Americans still had adolescent concerns such as the desire to stand out and shine, while their government indulged in adolescent behavior like saber rattling and brinkmanship.

His two-year stay in India in the 1960s brought him direct familiarity with spiritual traditions that young people in the United States and Europe were becoming increasingly enthusiastic about. Not only did he get a taste of what Eastern philosophy and spiritual practice had to offer, but he also gained insights while in India about the implications of spirituality for social and political philosophy. insights that he clearly put to good use in writing *The Spiritual Imperative.*

This spiritual orientation helped him to overcome the limitations of much Marxist thought in which changes in the institutional structure are seen as the key to social progress. He understood that without a raising of consciousness, social transformation would not occur. Of course, feminists had emphasized the need to raise consciousness and the identity of the personal and the political dimensions. His involvement in the radical feminist movement and close friendship with Shulamith Firestone in the late 1960s was a big step in his realizing the importance of inner transformation, but his Indian experience gave this conviction much greater depth and solidity.

Around this same period, he spent time on a kibbutz in Israel which showed him the benefits of cooperative economic life in decentralized communities that were based not on centuries-old traditions but on modern socialist ideals. He incorporated what he learned from this experience into his picture of the societies that would emerge during the new spiritual-religious era: decentralization, voluntary simplicity, and equality consciousness.

And for imagining the future, what better place to be than Japan where he spent almost all of the 1970s and 1980s. He had a ringside seat from which to take notes on Japan's quest to catch up with and exceed the United States economically. He made financial ends meet by teaching English at Japanese corporations and translating their documents. But most of all, he talked to people and had many friends both Japanese and foreign which helped him keep up with the main trends both inside and outside Japan, even though he did not do a lot of reading on these subjects. But he never became a Japanophile nor wanted to live out the rest of his life in Japan. Although his reading ability of Japanese was quite good, his spoken Japanese never progressed to the point where he could have stimulating intellectual discussions in Japanese. His Japanese friends were usually English-speaking and that was the language he used with them.

This brings us to one of the keys to his life. There was always a tension between his cosmopolitan outlook and his firmly held belief that ethnic identity is primary. Until he was past 65, he did not attempt to become part of a local community and establish a secure and stable position in a particular place. Instead, he moved around frequently, like the proverbial wandering Jew. Only toward the end of his life did he settle in Israel when he embraced his ethnic identity with alacrity, but it was too late for him to live out his days in peace and comfort. It wasn't easy to culturally assimilate, his Hebrew language ability was not that of a native speaker, and he never made close enough connections with people to banish his loneliness.

Taub kept up his spirits with the hope that *The Spiritual Imperative* would bring him recognition. He tried to sell the book and promote his ideas, until the lack of success wore him down and alcohol became a way out of his sorrow. Although he ultimately fell short in getting his life together, his unique work on universal history demonstrates that he saw and understood much of the world and took great pleasure in the human drama. Not bad for a working-class kid from Newark, New Jersey!

Part 5
The Spiritual Imperative Review
by Takuya Mirata

Source Citation: Murata, Takuya. "The Spiritual, Imperative: Sex, Age and the Last Caste. (Book review)." Futures 39.4 (May 2007)

Lawrence Taub makes a prediction about a course of events that are likely to happen. Following today's US power, China, Korea, and Japan will form a Confucianism-based Bloc to dominate the early 21st century. Then, this period of Far Eastern supremacy will be unraveled by the Middle East and South Asia-- the religious belt. Israel, the Middle East and India will rise as a Bloc to lead the Religious era, overcoming inter-faith differences. Finally, Africa and Indigenous peoples will take the torch in the later 21st century. This completes the human voyage and gives way to the superhuman age.

His prediction is not necessarily bright for the US. If Taub is right, the US will fall to the third place in the early 21st century, as a member of a north polar Bloc with Russia, and will not maintain its preeminent position as world leader. Given this prediction, he offers advice for the US to remain as competitive as possible. Taub's advice is to imitate Japan while it is still in the current era advantageous to the Confucian ethos, but not to imitate Japan so much that the US becomes too like Japan in a deep way, as this era will give way to another very soon. Taking the Japanese recession since 1989 into consideration, it seems more cogent to replace Japan with China, but either way Taub's argument seems to be that both these countries belong to the Confucian Bloc.

The author's prediction is based primarily on the caste model. Derived from Hindu philosophy, the caste model explains human history as one cycle of five ages: religious-spiritual, warrior, merchant, worker, and finally a return to another religious-spiritual age. This last age will differ in important ways from its first manifestation and coincides with the first stage of superhumanity. According to the author, superhumanity is something that no human being can at present understand. He illustrates this by an evolutionary comparison: chimpanzees cannot understand human civilization. It is praiseworthy to go out on a limb and predict a post-human world, but the lack of discussion of what that world might be like is a shortcoming of the book. Another weakness in unconventional thinking is that the book is bound to Earth: the author does not consider possibilities wherein humans progress to interplanetary migrations.

The core argument of this book on macrohistory rests on Taub's caste model. It needs elucidation in a little more detail. These five ages indicate the single most crucial determinant in global power. In the warrior age, symbolized by the Spanish and Portuguese empires, war and conquest were central. That age when kings and generals ruled changed into the merchant age. The British, and later the US, dominated this latter period when the world revolved around money and business. Currently we are living in the midst of the Worker Age, which means that one's profession is of predominant importance. The author explains that when you ask who someone is, most people will name their work--a doctor or a fire fighter--as a sense of being. Also, the Worker Age is also characterized by team effort which manifests itself internationally through nations working together as a team. There are many examples, from the European Union, ASEAN to the Organization of African States, as distinct from the former British, French or Japanese empires. Taub argues that the Confucian Bloc is most suited to this age due to their particular work ethic. The world keeps changing and people will tire of their endless labor as cogs in the machine. Thus, this worker age will be followed by a two-step religious-spiritual age in which religion and later, inner spirituality, will be of more fundamental value than money or work. In the religious-spiritual age, Israel, the Middle East and South Asia will assume leadership as the major religions of the world were born there: Judaism, Christianity, Islam and Buddhism. The author does not present empirical data to prove that the Confucians have a stronger work ethic than, say, the Calvinists of northern Europe. Mexican immigrants to the US work tirelessly for long hours, and yet Latinos are often stereotyped as lazy. I find the statement that citizens of the Confucian-influenced nations work harder than any other nation hard to accept. Even if this were true, there would still seem to be a tension between the teamwork ethic of the Worker Age and the Confucian essence which is frequently described as hierarchical.

My sense is that Taub's caste model will make many futurists think of the Prabhat Sarkar's model, articulated by Sohail Inayatullah in Macrohistory and Macrohistorians. This is probably due to three reasons. First, Sarkar's model also derives from Indian philosophy. Sarkar was born in an Indian family with regional leadership and connections to spiritual traditions. He went on to lead a spiritual-social movement in his adult life. Second, both models are based on the concept that a dominant feature characterizes each Age which moves in a cycle. Finally, both models ascribe the cause that makes one Age pass to the next to the disintegration of the age itself rather than an external force.

There are also important differences between the two models. In Sarkar's model the Ages move in a cycle and continue through history. Taub, on the other hand, thinks that while the world goes through many cycles, humans only go through this cycle once. Thus the first Age of the humans was the chimpanzees' last, and the last human Age coincides with the first superhuman one. In this way, Taub's model combines the linear and cyclical in a unique manner. To illustrate, for Sarkar, humans engage in numerous cycles of the Worker, Warrior, Intellectual and Capitalist ages, but in contrast, according to Taub, humans evolve cyclically from their first age, the Spiritual-Religious age, through the Warrior, Merchant and Worker ages to enter the final Religious-Spiritual age.

As today is the Worker Age, in Taub's view, the Religious-Spiritual Age should follow next. By this logic, events relating to religion and spirituality should be currently emerging issues. This does seem to be happening globally in different ways. The Islamic Revolution of 1979 occurred against the secularizing trend of both Capitalism and Communism. In the 1990s, the collapse of the secular Soviet Union was followed by the return of Muslim practices to Central Asia. We are indeed seeing the emergence of religious political groups, for instance, the Christian Right in Europe and the US and the BJP in India. Needless to say, Islamic Fundamentalism has become a household word post-9/11; but there many varieties of religious Fundamentalism. Taub's prediction fits at the intersection of the global re-emergence of religion and the social search for meaning in this increasingly consumerist world.

While we see conflicts between institutionalized religions, the Religious part of the Age will give way to the coming Spiritual part: a peaceful and equal world where people only need to work 4 h a week. According to the author, humanity has evolved to include more and more people in its circle of wealth, away from kings and despots ruling poor peasants into one where a significant number of people enjoy job security and relative freedom. He predicts this macro-trend will continue, until everyone will have enough and be able to live in security.

In our immediately real world, however, the debate about the economics effects of globalization continues. Does it raise all boats, small and big, or does it ruthlessly create poverty at a global scale? And in the developed world, we are seeing job security disappear before our eyes. Increasing unemployment in Europe, labor flexibility and layoffs introduced to Japan, and most recently, massive youth protests in France seem to point in the opposite direction from Taub. This is a classic emerging issue. Few people paid attention in 1974 when the post-Fordist economy arrived with flexible employment, and now, lack of security has turned into a powerful trend. In the short term, it seems that living standards are converging downwards and even fewer have access to economic security. On the other hand, even though living standards appear to be falling in the first world, there are signs that living standards are rising for some others. The emergence of a substantial middle class in China and India is one example. Separated from these dynamic changes, the world poor continue to live their lives of hardship, while some scholars count more poor people and others less.

In an effort to look beyond these complex and confusing surface events, and to dig below the extension and extrapolation from current trends, the author focuses on deep structures. For example, the author claims that Confucian cultural similarity between Japan, China and the Koreas, an ancient shared attribute, trumps the more recent divisions since World War II followed by Japan and South Korea's capitalist Americanization and China and North Korea's communist revolution. At one level, this argument seems spurious and essentialist. Can a Confucian identity march through history unchanged by these radical events? What is fresh about Taub's thesis is the present similarity he finds in China and Japan beyond the cultural level. He argues that the value of teamwork crosscuts both Japan's teamwork Capitalism and Chinese Communism.

A good reason to challenge macrohistories which posit ancient civilizations as the primary determinant is that they expunge individual agency. Individual choices and decisions become inconsequential in the predetermined story of fate. Individual choice does matter at least as much if not more than 'grand narrative' civilizational ones. Many unforeseen possibilities await us in the future.

The main weakness of this book is its two undeveloped models: the age model and sex model. The author does not discuss these models beyond introducing them in the first few chapters. Taub's predictions of the future, in which different blocs rise and fall, are almost entirely based on the caste model. But let us attend to the age model for a moment. It is based on the notion that "the life of humanity as a whole parallels the life of a single individual." From this age model, Taub assigns ages to regions: the Netherlands and Scandinavia are 25 years old, the US and Western Europe 19 and Indigenous peoples in infancy or early childhood. The rest of the world, namely Asia, Africa and South America, is 13. Iran (Mesopotamia), India and China, some of the most ancient civilizations, are said to be young, while the Europeans and the US which is a very new nation built in 1776, are said to be more adult. I found this age assignment somewhat surprising and would have liked more explanation why this is the case.

But even taking these age assignments at face value, there seems to be a more basic logical flaw. Taub declares that the most mature humans have only grown to age 25 since 4000BC but that human beings will evolve into superhumanity by the later 21st century. If we matured only 25 years in more than 6000 years, it is unclear how humanity is expected to age far more quickly to become superhumans in less than one hundred years. Taub does not discuss the age model beyond the stage of becoming adult. It is a model based on positivist logic. But if we heed natural law, humanity should not simply become adult and freeze in time. Rather, humanity's maturation from infancy to adulthood should be followed by middle and old age, until finally reaching death and potential rebirth as superhuman. It does not make sense that the adult stage in itself should coincide with the birth of the superhuman cycle.

Given the care and logical precision that Taub devotes to the caste model, he ought to be capable of fully developing the age and sex models which would give greater depth to his thinking on the future.

* * *

Part 6
Foreword to Japanese edition
by Masanori Kanda

What? Alvin Toffler is living in Tokyo? That's the thought that went through my mind when I finished reading the last page of this book. Even if it wasn't Alvin Toffler, Peter Drucker or John Kenneth Galbraith would have been just as good comparisons. The point is, what surprised me was the fact that a Westerner, with a fine and noble mind equal to that of the great thinkers of history, has been living in Tokyo for many years, quietly, and without anyone being aware of it.

Lawrence Taub. I gradually became firmly convinced that this unknown author, when we consider this book, his maiden work, is as worthy as those great thinkers who have carved their name into history. Right at the start, the title itself of the original book hit me with great impact. *The Spiritual Imperative: Sex, Age, and the Last Caste* (which Mr. Kanda here translates literally into Japanese). According to Taub, sex, age, and caste, three seemingly completely unconnected principles, can explain human history and the future.

This bold hypothesis is interesting if you are sitting around talking and drinking. But serious people are not supposed to take it seriously. And to be honest, when I first picked up the original book, I turned its pages with suspicion. As I feared, the book's content flies off in all directions through human time and space. As if I were in a time machine, the book let me observe at a glance all time from about 3000 B.C.E in the distant past to the year 2150 in the future. And as if I were looking down at the Earth from a satellite, my eyes roamed east and west, north and south, from Europe and North and South America to Asia, the Middle East, and Africa.

Further, the book discusses everything from sex to the international political system and currencies in a single straight line. So that the further along I read the more I felt as if my brain was being stretched to its limits. Yet though the book is so comprehensive and covers such a wide area, and the discussion unfolds before and below you like an abyss, it's never hard to understand. It's more as if you were reading a mystery or detective story; you find yourself turning the pages faster and faster.

And it's a book that gives the reader, once he or she finishes reading it, that sense of refreshing exhilaration and of being touched to the heart that you feel after seeing a high-quality movie. Among the many books around that make future forecasts, what's so special about this one is that, though it covers thousands of years of human history, it explains the present, all the things we observe happening in front of our eyes that seem to make no sense at all to us, in a way that makes them seem perfectly rational and logical. And it explains these things in a clear and beautiful way using three basic concepts, or "principles", that we would never think of using for such a purpose: sex, age, and caste. It makes clear to us, for example:

- Why men are piercing their ears and the rest of their bodies, putting on makeup, in short, "feminizing" themselves.
- Why China, which until now has been uniformly anti-Japanese, has suddenly been switching to a pro-Japanese line.
- Why the "spiritual boom" of recent years shows no signs of letting up.
- Why, despite the constantly decreasing birthrate, the education business continues to grow.

- Why the environmental issue, although the scientific basis for it is to some extent criticized as being vague, has become everyday common sense.
- Why homosexuality and adultery are constantly on the increase, while the "normal" conventional view of marriage and family gets shakier and shakier.

Taub's models make clear that these hard-to-explain everyday events and trends are actually inevitable, because they lead to the next inevitable stage in human evolution. So the scene we are observing is changing to a completely different one right before our eyes. No longer are we forced to live troubled and discordant lives based on a value system divorced from reality. Instead we can choose to live our lives on the path that leads to a new value system just now under construction.

This raises the question, how is it that Mr. Taub, focused on delving deep into human history, could come up with such models that, though quite unusual, he can use to explain even everyday events? The answer, now that I think of it, was already there, though not easily apparent, the day I first met him.

The date was June 22, 2006. He and I had made an appointment to meet at a café on a side street just off Omotesando, in the Harajuku area of Tokyo. I imagined he would turn out to be one of those fussy, fastidious scholars, but instead, there he appeared, a small rucksack on his back and a pipe in his mouth. Although he had been living in Tokyo for decades, he seemed like a traveler who had just casually dropped into one more country. The pupils of his eyes moved a lot, like those of a child, which impressed me. And he seemed really overjoyed when suddenly, in the middle of our conversation, a call came in on his cell phone from a friend.

Mr. Taub phoned many times after our appointment that day, speaking not only with me, but also with employees at my company. These conversations always seemed effortless and enjoyable. Whenever he called to ask advice about something that was troubling him, or whenever a relevant question came up about some topic that interested him, he seemed to forget about time and talk about it with enthusiasm and without pretensions.

Mr. Taub is neither an ivory-tower type buried deep in old books nor a top-level figure in the worlds of politics or finance, whom everybody addresses as "sensei, sensei." While leading an ordinary life (though "ordinary" is the most difficult thing of all), he continues his explorations of the world, human life, and space, wondering what will be. Paying no attention to a person's status or national origin, and loving the people right in front of his eyes at the moment equally, he continues searching for the meaning of being alive, wondering what will happen.

This is something that spreads across the deep strata of this book, the thing that no sage or wise man before could ever acquire – the knowledge of the Trickster.

Yet why was he living for decades in Japan?

At the time the decision was made to publish this book here in Japan, I remembered wanting to ask him this question again. Just when I decided to get together with him again to do that, I got a phone call from him on my cell phone. He was calling from Narita Airport. I could envision his usual smiling face as we talked.

"I'll be away from Japan and am going to Israel for a while." With those parting words he left Japan.

How long was "for a while?" A half year? Twenty or thirty years? He didn't know either. Probably his stay in Israel will last until he is sure that history is reaching the turning point.

When that historical turning point that he foresaw actually happens, his reputation will no longer be in doubt, and his name will be up there with the leading thinkers of history. And we here in Japan will take pride in the fact that Taub-san lived in Japan for so long.

That pride that Japan will feel will be similar to the pride it feels in having been the first country to value and adopt Edward Deming's Quality Control methods and principles and in the fact that Albert Einstein was in mid-ocean, heading for Japan, when he received the Nobel Prize.

Masanori Kanda

Epilogue

Taub conceived the ideas for his macrohistory in the late 1970s, and though forty years have passed, many of his forecasts remain relevant, while others have not stood the test of time.

For instance, Taub predicted the formation of new economic unions, envisioning a bloc called "Confucio" between China, Japan, and Korea, and another named "Polario" comprising North America, Russia, and the Nordic countries. Both predictions are unrealistic today.

What Taub did not foresee are the geopolitical shifts triggered by the war in Ukraine, which have redefined global alliances. The rise of BRICS, fueled by these disruptions, has made the realization of Polario or Confucio unlikely, at least for the foreseeable future.

But Taub's remarkable feat was to map the Varna cycle to actual human history. In doing so, he conceptually integrated Eastern cyclical and Western linear views of time.

In Vedic thought, humanity goes through the Varna cycle that leads to a new spiritual age, after which the cycle starts anew. Monotheistic traditions follow a linear progression, from the Garden of Eden to the Second Coming. They take different paths but the destination is the same.

In his later years, Taub resided in Jerusalem, a city steeped in monotheistic conflict. Living on the fault line between Islam and Judaism, he believed he had discerned how the centuries-old tensions between the two faiths would be resolved.

According to his Sex Model, both Islam and Judaism were excessively masculine (or "yang"). Taub predicted that women, embodying feminine ("yin") traits such as compromise, empathy, and cooperation, would eventually restore balance between the two peoples. He envisioned Jewish and Arab women drawing inspiration from biblical figures, Sarah and Hagar to bridge the divide between them. In *The Spiritual Imperative* he wrote:

"The Biblical story in Genesis of Abraham, Sarah, and Hagar, forms the basis for the belief that the Jews and Arabs are blood-related. In the story, Abraham's beloved wife, Sarah, was infertile. To continue the family line, she "gave" Abraham her Egyptian maidservant, Hagar, for the job of childbearing.

But Sarah got jealous and treated Hagar badly. Hagar ran away and later gave birth to her son by Abraham, Ishmael. God blessed Hagar and Ishmael, enabling them to survive. Later, when Sarah was double the normal childbearing age limit, she became fertile and bore a son, Isaac.

The Jews and Arabs both believe that Ishmael was the ancestor of the Arabs and that Isaac was the ancestor of the Jews — that the two peoples are, therefore, "half-brothers and -sisters," both descended from Father Abraham.

Once the patriarchal dominion over the Arabs and the Jews has been broken, Jewish and Arab women will come together and say: "The land is as much Hagar's as Sarah's. Both peoples have inherited it. Let us weaken the patriarchy and affirm the sisterhood of our foremothers by reconciling their ancient squabble. Let us bring the two halves of the family together by sharing the land, bonding spiritually, and working together to achieve a prosperity that will make both our peoples strong."

* * *

Diagrams from *The Spiritual Imperative*

THE FOUR BASIC CASTES OF THE WORLD

CASTE	RELIGIOUS-SPIRITUAL	WARRIOR	MERCHANT	WORKER
Sanskrit Name	Brahman	Kshattriya	Vaishva	Shudra
World View	God, Enlightenment	Combat, Competition	Money, Material Possessions	Identification with Work, Skill, Job, Sci-Tech Knowledge, Company
Ruling Elite	<u>Pre- and Early History</u>: Shamans, Witches, High Priests and Popes <u>The Future</u>: Top Religious and Spiritual Leaders	Kings, Emperors, Top Nobility and Generals	Top Capitalists, Traders, Industrialists, Financiers and Landowners	Top technocrats and bureaucrats in the top private and public enterprises, government, parties, and labor organizations
Skills, Tools and Institutions	Religious Rituals, Churches, Mosques, Synagogues, Temples, etc.; Spiritual Practices, including Martial Arts	Armies, Strategies, and Weapons	Trade, Finance, Banking, Transportation, Communication, Industry, Sci-Tech, Entrepreneur-run Companies	Agricultural, Blue-collar, and White-collar Jobs, Skills, and Expertise; High Technology; and Bureaucratic organizations. The CEO-run Corporation
Social Ideal	The Religious Leader and the Enlightened Soul	The Hero	The Self-Made Man	The Organization Man/The *Sarariman*
Source of Power	<u>Pre- and Early History</u>: Religious Knowledge <u>The Future</u>: Self-Knowledge	Land	Capital	Scientific, Technical and Managerial Knowledge
Economic-Political Unit	<u>Pre- and Early History</u>: The Tribe <u>The Future</u>: The Kibbutz, Moshav, Community	The Petty Empire	The Grand Empire	The Economic-Political Bloc

CLASS STRUCTURES OF THE FOUR CASTES

FIG. 2

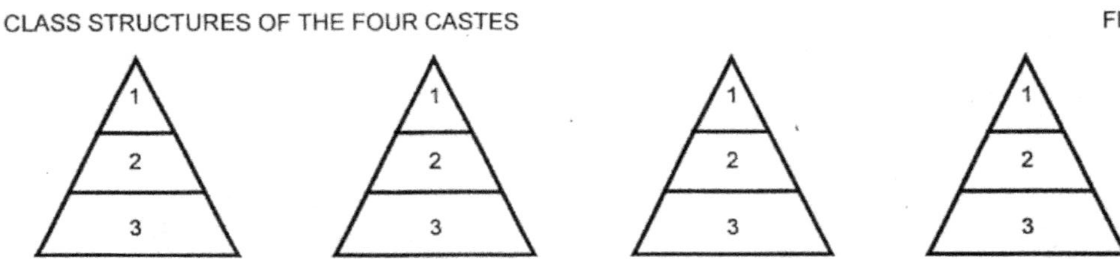

Pyramids indicate that the lower down in the caste you are, the greater the number of people.

WARRIOR	MERCHANT	WORKER	RELIGIOUS-SPIRITUAL
1. Top kings, emperors, generals, and nobility	1. Grande bourgeoisie: top entrepreneurs, capitalists, industrialists, landlords, and financiers	1. The bureau-technostructure: top executives, sci-technicians, professionals, administrators, government and party bureaucrats, labor leaders	1. Top level leaders, gurus, rabbis, ayatollahs, popes, archbishops, etc. of organized religions as well as powerful charismatic sect/group/public spiritual and religious leaders unaffiliated with traditional organized religions
2. Middle-rank kings, nobles, knights, samurai, and military officers	2. Entrepreneurs, traders, capitalists, factory owners, landlords, and financiers who own and run smaller businesses and landholdings	2. Middle-level executives, professionals, administrators, bureaucrats, sci-technicians, party cadres, and academics	2. Less influential people of the above type
3. 'Cannon-fodder' level: vast hordes of ordinary knights, samurai and soldiers	3. 'Pettiest' bourgeoisie: streets full of powerless small shopkeepers and traders	3. Worker armies of white- and blue-collar and agricultural 'wage slaves', unemployed, and homeless	3. The rank-and-file active members of traditional religions and sects and of spiritual, 'new-age' and other sects and groups unaffiliated with traditional, organized religion

THE CASTE MODEL

FIG. 3

THE FIVE CASTE AGES	SANSKRIT NAME	TIME
(animal)		
1. Spiritual-Religious Age No. 1	Satyayuga I	3 million to 4000/2000 BC
2. Warrior Age	Tretayuga	4000/2000 BC to early 17th Century AD
3. Merchant Age	Dvaparayuga	c. 1650 to c. 1975
4. Worker Age	Kaliyuga	c. 1917 to c. 2030
5. Spiritual-Religious Age No. 2	Satyayuga II	c. 1979 to Superhumanity
(superhuman)		

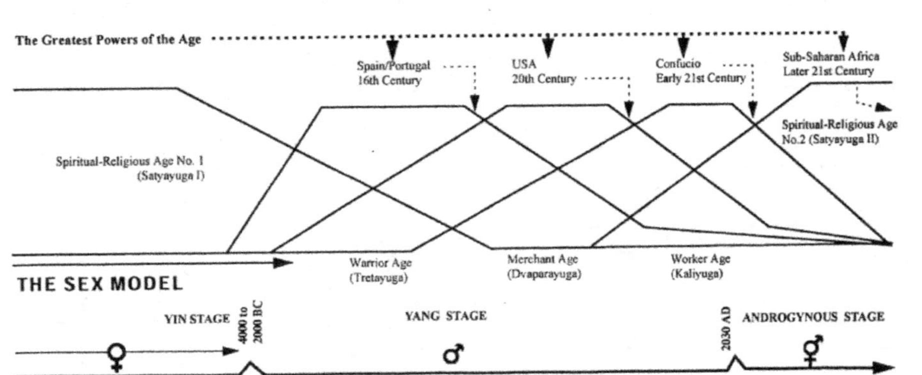

THE SEX MODEL

THREE STAGES OF A CASTE'S RISE TO POWER

FIG. 4

STAGE	DEFINITION: WHAT HAPPENS	GEOGRAPHICAL LOCATION: WHERE IT HAPPENS
1. Pioneering Stage	The rising caste organizes and sets up pockets of power and opposition/resistance to the caste in power, but does not rule anywhere yet.	This stage unfolds in the main centers of world power, i.e., those countries/regions in which the ruling caste is most powerful and from which it rules the rest of the world: the Great Powers ('First World').
2. Revolutionary-Evolutionary Stage	The rising caste takes power in some countries through revolutions – bourgeois, socialist or religious, depending on the caste age. These countries become the new 'Second World' challenging great powers. But at the same time, the rising caste takes power even in those countries which are the main centers of world power – the 'First World' established great powers – but by *evolution* rather than revolution.	The revolutions unfold *outside* the main centers of world power, in certain 'backward', 'Third World' countries/regions. But the rising caste's *evolutionary* takeovers of power unfold in the same countries – the main centers of world power – in which its pioneering stage unfolded.
3. Peak Stage	The rising caste is now at the height of its world power, rules the world – and is about to fall.	This stage unfolds in those countries/regions which have evolved to be most in tune with the spirit and world view of the rising caste. These are the countries which therefore most 'belong' to that caste, and thus become the new great powers – the 'First World' – of that caste age.

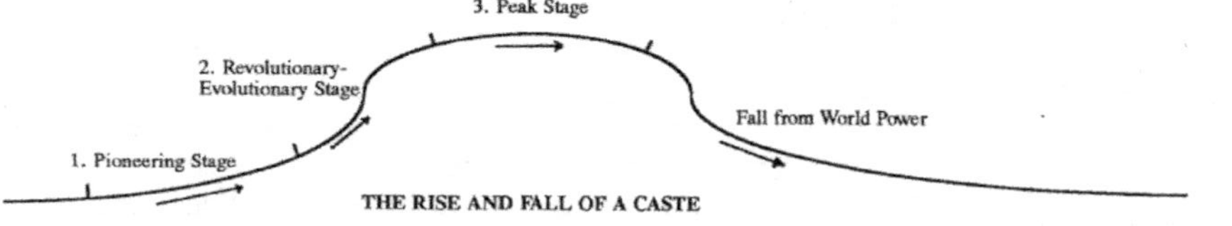

THE SEX DIALECTIC

FIG. 5

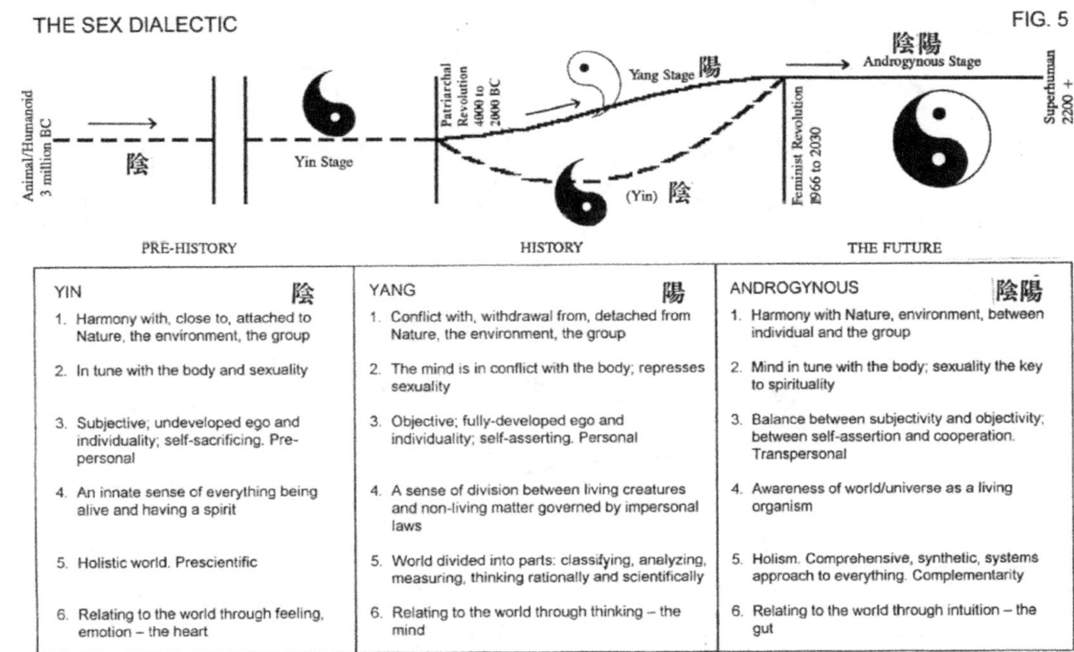

YIN 陰	YANG 陽	ANDROGYNOUS 陰陽
1. Harmony with, close to, attached to Nature, the environment, the group	1. Conflict with, withdrawal from, detached from Nature, the environment, the group	1. Harmony with Nature, environment, between individual and the group
2. In tune with the body and sexuality	2. The mind is in conflict with the body; represses sexuality	2. Mind in tune with the body; sexuality the key to spirituality
3. Subjective; undeveloped ego and individuality; self-sacrificing. Pre-personal	3. Objective; fully-developed ego and individuality; self-asserting. Personal	3. Balance between subjectivity and objectivity; between self-assertion and cooperation. Transpersonal
4. An innate sense of everything being alive and having a spirit	4. A sense of division between living creatures and non-living matter governed by impersonal laws	4. Awareness of world/universe as a living organism
5. Holistic world. Prescientific	5. World divided into parts: classifying, analyzing, measuring, thinking rationally and scientifically	5. Holism. Comprehensive, synthetic, systems approach to everything. Complementarity
6. Relating to the world through feeling, emotion – the heart	6. Relating to the world through thinking – the mind	6. Relating to the world through intuition – the gut

FIG. 6
SEXO-CULTURAL DIVISION OF THE WORLD INTO
THE YANGER WEST AND THE YINNER EAST
Yin World Religions
Hinduism
Buddhism
Yin 陰
Yang 陽 Yang
Benares
The Female Pole
Jerusalem
The Male Pole
Yang World Religions
Judaism
Christianity
Islam

THE AGE MODEL

FIG. 7

(The Life of Humanity Evolves Parallel to the Life of a Single Person)

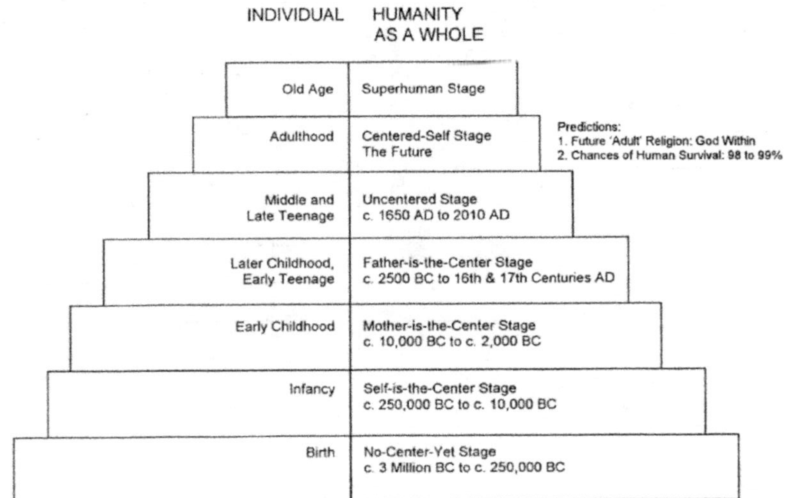

THE RISE OF THE MERCHANT CASTE

(The Merchant Age)

FIG. 8

STAGE	WHAT HAPPENED	WHERE IT HAPPENED	WHEN IT HAPPENED
1. Pioneering Stage	The merchant caste - loosely, the bourgeoisie – set up bases of power and opposition to warrior caste - loosely, the kings and nobility - rule.	The Holy Roman Empire and Central Europe, esp. the North Italian City States and the Hanseatic League.	12th to 16th Centuries AD
2. Revolutionary-Evolutionary Stage	'Bourgeois' revolutions or their equivalent broke out in countries in Europe, North America and Japan, bringing the merchant caste to power in these countries... ...while the merchant caste also slowly took power - by evolution rather than by revolution - even in those advanced countries that did not experience such revolutions.	The 'Bourgeois' Revolutions were: 1. Dutch Revolution against Spain, 1567 to 1609 2. British Revolution (Civil War) of 1649 to 1660 3. American Revolution, 1776 4. French Revolution, 1789 5. 2nd American Revolution (Civil War), 1861 to 1865 6. German Unification, 1871 7. Meiji Restoration of Japan, 1867	16th to 19th Centuries AD
3. Peak Stage	The United States, the country that most 'belonged' to the merchant caste - that was most in tune with its spirit and world view of money and material wealth - became the world's greatest power.	The United States of America was the No. 1 World Power	c. 1942 to c. 1980

THE RISE OF THE WORKER CASTE

(The Worker Age)

FIG. 9

STAGE	WHAT HAPPENED	WHERE IT HAPPENED	WHEN IT HAPPENED
1. Pioneering Stage	The blue-collar segment of the worker caste organized to resist the merchant caste: utopian socialist communities; socialist, anarchist, and communist movements and political parties; trade unions; and unsuccessful uprisings.	The advanced industrialized countries of the time: Western Europe, North America, Japan, Australia, New Zealand, South Africa, etc.	19th and early 20th Centuries
2. Revolutionary-Evolutionary Stage	Socialist-communist revolution replaced 'bourgeois' revolution as the main form of revolution... ...while the worker caste continued to take power – by evolution rather than by revolution – even in the advanced industrialized countries. Results of both revolutionary and evolutionary trends: The upper – white-collar – echelon of the worker caste, the technocratic-bureaucratic 'new class' elite, gained power in all these countries.	Socialist-communist revolutions succeeded in 'backward' countries *outside* the main centers of world power: Russia, Mongolia, China, Yugoslavia, North Korea, Vietnam, Cuba, Laos, Cambodia, and Nicaragua.	1917 to 1979
3. Peak Stage	Confucio, the cultural-economic-political bloc that most 'belongs' to the worker caste – that is most in tune with its spirit of identification with work, job, technical knowledge, and company – will become the world's greatest power of the age.	Confucio – consisting of Japan, China, Taiwan, Hong Kong, Macao, North and South Korea – will be the No. 1 World Power.	1979 to c. 2040

Edited by Jan Krikke

PEAK STAGE OF THE WORKER AGE

Division of the World into Economic/Political Blocs (from 1950s to c. 2030 AD)

FIG. 10

1. Confucio (No. 1 World Power) – consisting of China (incl. Taiwan, Hong Kong, and Macao), Korea (North and South reunified), Japan

2. Europa (No. 2 World Power) – consisting of Eastern and Western Europe (minus CIS countries and possibly Scandinavia)

3. Polario (No 3 World Power) – consisting of USA, Russia plus non-Islamic CIS countries, Canada, possibly Scandinavia and Mexico

4. ASEAN – Thailand, Philippines, Singapore, Malaysia, Indonesia, Brunei, Vietnam, Laos, Cambodia, Burma

5. Latin American Blocs

6. African Blocs

7. Oceanian Bloc – Australia, New Zealand, Pacific nations

POLARIO
The polar map at the left illustrates that the four giant countries/regions that will make up Polario are neighbours around the North Pole.

THE RISE OF THE RELIGIOUS-SPIRITUAL CASTE

(The Spiritual-Religious Age No. 2)

FIG. 11

The four great powers of the 'Religious Belt' – the new top world powers of the mid-21st century, emerging as a result of religious revolution during the Revolutionary-Evolutionary Stage of this age – will be:

1. South Asian, or Bharati, Federation
2. Central Asian Islamic Federation
3. Pan-Semitic Federation
4. Maghreb Federation

PIONEERING STAGE (1950S THROUGH 1970S)

Unfolded in all the advanced industrialized countries, including Western Europe, North America, Japan, Korea, Eastern Europe, the Soviet Union, Israel, Australia, New Zealand, and the developed regions of the South.

REVOLUTIONARY-EVOLUTIONARY STAGE (FROM 1979 TO C. 2050)

This stage started with the Islamic Revolution in Iran in 1979. The nature of revolution changes from socialist to religious revolution. Religious revolutions will continue to break out in the 'Religious Belt' stretching from Bangladesh across India, the Middle East to North Africa (see Map).

In all these countries, there has been a return to the established/traditional religions of humanity's 'childhood-adolescence' as well as a groping forward to a new type of spirituality, unaffiliated with traditional/organized religions and sects, that will eventually become the 'adult' God-within spirituality of the future foreseen by the Age Model.

PEAK STAGE (c. 2050 to c. 2100 plus)

The most influential region in the world will be Sub-Saharan – Black – Africa.